Transformation to Performance Excellence

Also available from ASQ Quality Press:

The Quality Rubric: A Systematic Approach for Implementing Quality Principles and Tools in Classrooms and Schools
Steve Benjamin

The Principal's Leadership Counts! Launch a Baldrige-Based Quality School
Margaret A. Byrnes with Jeanne C. Baxter

There Is Another Way! Launch a Baldrige-Based Quality Classroom
Margaret A. Byrnes with Jeanne C. Baxter

Charting Your Course: Lessons Learned During the Journey Toward Performance Excellence
John G. Conyers and Robert Ewy

Quality Across the Curriculum: Integrating Quality Tools and PDSA with Standards
Jay Marino and Ann Haggerty Raines

Permission to Forget: And Nine Other Root Causes of America's Frustration with Education
Lee Jenkins

Smart Teaching: Using Brain Research and Data to Continuously Improve Learning
Ronald J. Fitzgerald

Improving Student Learning: Applying Deming's Quality Principles in the Classroom, 2nd Edition
Lee Jenkins

Successful Applications of Quality Systems in K–12 Schools
The ASQ Quality Education Division

Futuring Tools for Strategic Quality Planning in Education
William F. Alexander and Richard W. Serfass

Insights to Performance Excellence 2006: An Inside Look at the 2006 Baldrige Award Criteria
Mark L. Blazey

Thinking Tools for Kids: An Activity Book for Classroom Learning
Barbara A. Cleary and Sally J. Duncan

To request a complimentary catalog of ASQ Quality Press publications, call 800-248-1946, or visit our Web site at http://qualitypress.asq.org.

Transformation to Performance Excellence

Baldrige Education Leaders Speak Out

Sandra Cokeley, APR
Director of Quality and Community Relations, Pearl River School District; ASQ Education Advisory Committee Chair

Margaret A. Byrnes
Managing Associate, Quality Education Associates;
ASQ Education Division Vice-Chair K–12

Geri Markley
Executive Director, Michigan Quality Council;
Assistant Professor and Chair, Cleary University;
ASQ Education Division Chair Elect

Suzanne Keely, CQIA
ASQ Market Manager, Education

ASQ Quality Press
Milwaukee, Wisconsin

American Society for Quality, Quality Press, Milwaukee 53203

Printed in the United States of America
12 11 10 09 08 07 06   5 4 3 2 1

Library of Congress Cataloging-in-Publication Data

Transformation to performance excellence : Baldrige education leaders speak out / [editing team, Sandra Cokeley . . . et al.].
p. cm.
ISBN-13: 978-0-87389-697-9 (paper back)
1. Total quality management in education—United States. 2. School improvement programs—United States. 3. Malcolm Baldrige National Quality Award. I. Cokeley, Sandra, 1956–

LB2806.T685 2006
371.200973—dc22

2006029670

Publisher: William A. Tony
Acquisitions Editor: Matt Meinholz
Project Editor: Paul O'Mara
Production Administrator: Randall Benson

ASQ Mission: The American Society for Quality advances individual, organizational, and community excellence worldwide through learning, quality improvement, and knowledge exchange.

Attention Bookstores, Wholesalers, Schools, and Corporations: ASQ Quality Press books, videotapes, audiotapes, and software are available at quantity discounts with bulk purchases for business, educational, or instructional use. For information, please contact ASQ Quality Press at 800-248-1946, or write to ASQ Quality Press, P.O. Box 3005, Milwaukee, WI 53201-3005.

To place orders or to request a free copy of the ASQ Quality Press Publications Catalog, including ASQ membership information, call 800-248-1946. Visit our Web site at www.asq.org or http://qualitypress.asq.org.

Quality Press
600 N. Plankinton Avenue
Milwaukee, Wisconsin 53203
Call toll free 800-248-1946
Fax 414-272-1734
www.asq.org
http://qualitypress.asq.org
http://standardsgroup.asq.org
E-mail: authors@asq.org

Printed on acid-free paper

Contents

Figures and Tables

Foreword

Baldrige is a system for managing and improving the focus on learning and student success for schools at all levels. To function well, a system needs senior leadership guidance, direction, commitment, and nurturing. A retrospective analysis of the application scoring of the recipients of the Malcolm Baldrige National Quality Award reveals that the single highest-performing and highest-scoring element in these organizations is their senior leadership.

Visionary Leadership is the first of the Baldrige 11 Core Values—embedded beliefs and behaviors found in high-performing organizations—and it is no accident that *Leadership* is also Category 1 in the Baldrige Education Criteria for Performance Excellence. It asks how senior leaders guide and sustain their organization, how they communicate with faculty and staff and encourage high performance, and how they serve as role models through their ethical behavior—behavior that reinforces values and expectations while building leadership, commitment, and initiative throughout the organization.

A retrospective analysis of the application scoring of the recipients of the Malcolm Baldrige National Quality Award reveals that the single highest-performing and highest-scoring element in these organizations is their senior leadership.

We are proud of these successful leaders and their organizations, and we value their service as ambassadors for the Baldrige program. I am confident that you will learn important lessons from them, and I hope that you will follow their leadership in taking your organization on your own Baldrige journey.

Harry S. Hertz, Director
Malcolm Baldrige National Quality Program

Introduction

The ancient Roman scholar Marcus Terentius Varro wrote that "the longest part of any journey is the passing of the gate." By opening this volume, you have elected to open the gate that represents how your organization currently operates and to gaze down the road toward performance excellence. There is a long, historical tradition of voyagers being inspired by the stories of those who have traveled before them. In these pages, you will have an opportunity to hear stories from the individuals from the seven educational organizations that have used the Baldrige Education Criteria for Performance Excellence as a guide along their route to designing and improving educational systems.

In our discussions with individuals from schools and education organizations, we at the American Society for Quality (ASQ) and the National Institute of Standards and Technology (NIST) have had many people ask us the questions you'll find in this book. We thought that leaders from the Baldrige Award education recipients—seven since 2001—were the best resources for answers to these questions. You will be reading these answers in their own words.

This is not a "How to Win the Baldrige Award" book. It doesn't explain the Criteria question by question. There are other books that do that. It doesn't give you the road map everyone would like to have, because there is not one road to follow. Reading Baldrige recipients' responses to the questions we most often hear is an opportunity to learn which roads they took and where it got them. It gives you an opportunity to think about what road you might take and what maps might help you.

It's important to understand that each leader took a little different path. Sometimes there was a detour involved, and the leaders learned something new along the way. They often had a hard time convincing others to believe that this was a journey worth taking, and they had to respond to questions such as: Why do I have to change the way I'm working? How can I focus on *this* with all these other things I absolutely have to do? Why should we use a business model when we're in education? You'll find answers to these types of resistance in the responses.

A major learning from our conversations is that it takes a unique leader with a strong vision to begin and stay on this journey. And that's what each of these seven individuals did. Each began his journey to performance excellence as a result of his organization's respective circumstances and is continuing it today. These individuals know the journey was worthwhile. They've learned a lot and have willingly shared.

Each of the seven leaders and his organization exemplify the core values and principles of the Baldrige Education Criteria for Performance Excellence: Visionary Leadership; Learning-Centered Education; Organizational and Personal Learning; Valuing Faculty, Staff, and Partners; Agility; Focus on the Future; Managing for Innovation; Management by Fact; Social Responsibility; Focus on Results and Creating Value; and Systems Perspective. These criteria are now embedded in the culture of these organizations. Many of these probably also operate in your own organization, and some are perhaps areas deserving of deeper exploration. You can find complete definitions of these values and principles in Appendix C of this book along with other resources.

The ASQ Education Advisory Committee, made up of educators from K–12 and higher education, discussed this book at length. They reviewed and agreed on the set of questions for these leaders to answer. These are very real questions, asked simply, and answered in varying degrees of detail. The question/answer format for this book was chosen because we wanted a book that was informal and easy to pick up and read in relation to where you are in your own journey. You can read it from cover to cover or randomly choose a question you are currently facing to see how these leaders responded.

We've also included a CD that has the Baldrige applications for each of these organizations. When the leaders' responses reference something about which you'd like to learn more, you can open the application document to see what was written in reference to that aspect of the Criteria. Each application includes an organizational profile, which will give you a great deal of information about the organization and where it was at that time. It gives the leaders' explanation of how they "live" each of the Criteria, and the results they attained because of it.

These seven people did not do this alone. It is not an individual journey. These leaders took those first steps and passed through the gate Marcus Terentius Varro wrote about so long ago. There were many who followed them through that gate—enthusiastically or somewhat reluctantly—but eventually they supported the vision of these leaders and made it possible to change how their organizations were operating. Though you will not hear them "speak" in this book, they are an important reason these organizations have achieved performance excellence.

We hope this book is useful for your own learning, whether you're new to the Baldrige principles or experienced in them. If you are not an educator but have a passion for performance excellence in education, share it with your favorite superintendent or university dean or president.

If you are a superintendent, a dean, or a university president, you may want to share it with your cabinet, your board, or your leadership team so they can also learn from these successes and experiences. They will see that there is no prescribed route for the journey to performance excellence. However you use this book, we hope it will encourage you to take those first or next steps. And we hope that there are some of you who will read this book and go on to provide the next round of stories that define performance excellence for educational systems.

Question 1

How did you get started using the Criteria? As a leader, do you use the Criteria on a daily basis? If so, how?

Answers

John Conyers; District 15 We got started by saying we as senior leaders were going to hold ourselves accountable to the Criteria. We modeled this resolution whenever we could to demonstrate that we were following up with our statements of accountability. We found that we weren't always aware that we were using the Criteria specifically, but it had become a core value of the district. You use the Baldrige Criteria daily because your customers or constituents want results that fit their idea of what quality is, not just occasionally, but consistently.

You use the Baldrige Criteria daily because your customers or constituents want results that fit their idea of what quality is, not just occasionally, but consistently.

Joe Alexander; Monfort As is the case with any organization that has attempted to implement Baldrige, there was a time where it was new and possibly even uncomfortable in that some of the terminology seemed foreign and many of the questions were downright difficult to address. Attempting to apply the Criteria was decidedly formal at that point, with specific task forces or committees set up to meet on a regular basis for the expressed purpose of working on the Baldrige application and identifying where things needed to be done differently in order to approach organizational solutions that better matched with the Criteria.

What happens over time is analogous to much of what we do as humans in that the more comfortable we get with a given set of tasks, the more they become a natural part of how we behave. While we are certainly not to the point as an organization where all of the Criteria are natural for us, I do think we are gradually moving to a point where we are doing things the Baldrige way without even being conscious at the time that that is what we are doing. To me, that's the ultimate goal.

What happens over time is analogous to much of what we do as humans in that the more comfortable we get with a given set of tasks, the more they become a natural part of how we behave.

Charles Sorensen; UW-Stout When we first considered applying for the Baldrige, we spent a day with a consultant—a UW-Stout graduate and examiner—reviewing each Criterion and the data used in each. Data collection, data analysis, and making data-driven decisions were common practices here. We realized quickly that while this was our practice, the Criteria provided a comprehensive way to review data, adopt a systems approach to understanding trends, and review processes and outcomes in a comprehensive way. After the first application, we realized that benchmarking against sister institutions or universities nationally allowed us to understand this university in a different fashion. We realized that we could actually demonstrate with data the simple fact that UW-Stout compared favorably in most categories, and we could see where improvements were necessary.

Within the first year after the initial application, we began to review, analyze, and use the data in a systematic, ongoing way. The Chancellor's Advisory Council (CAC), made up of members from each constituent group on campus and, in effect, the decision-making body for all fiscal issues, meets biweekly. Normally at these meetings we review some data set or subset to understand an issue more clearly. We review trends so we understand on a three-year basis how we are doing. This is particularly true if the trend lines are negative. This, I would add, is a great advantage to the Baldrige process: it forces an examination of issues whether they are positive or negative. And for many, if not most, institutions, understanding and analyzing negative trends is difficult and uncomfortable, but the Baldrige demands this if the health of the institution is to be understood.

This regular and consistent use of data has had a very positive impact on this campus. It has, in my opinion, changed the way we review and analyze data and plan for our future. We are a much more proactive campus, planning not only for the short term, but by understanding social and economic trends, willing to commit to long-range plans. With our eyes always on the data, always sensitive to trends, we have been able to clearly align our mission, vision, and our short- and longer-term priorities with our budget process. In fact, we never establish a priority unless we provide the budget for implementation.

Question 2

School boards are elected "bosses." How do you get them to buy in?

Answers

Kirby Lehman; Jenks The keys to good school board members are strong professional development and heavy involvement in decision making and goal development, and sometimes these keys go hand in hand. There are several methods for providing professional development for school board members. First, the state school board members' association is typically an ideal vehicle for providing such board development opportunities for rookie and veteran board members. Additionally, school district staff members can and should provide board development opportunities in areas where individual staff members have a high level of expertise. Perhaps most important in the board development process is the direct involvement of the board members in determining the school district's goals and strategic objectives. In our district we review

The keys to good school board members are strong professional development and heavy involvement in decision making and goal development, and sometimes these keys go hand in hand.

the district's goals and strategic objectives on an annual basis. We establish new goals and objectives on a biennial basis, although oftentimes some of the previous biennium's goals are carried forward.

Using a cadre of administrators to develop board members at school board retreats is a strategy we have employed. Additionally, we have isolated board members with outstanding curricular, instructional, or other strategies via curriculum showcases in the school district on a twice-annual basis, and these activities have proven to be excellent vehicles for board development. Using school board meetings for the purpose of providing routine opportunities for school board member development in very specific and isolated areas of student activities, curriculum areas, or instructional strategies has also worked well. Last, the superintendent's communications directly to school board members provide the vehicle for communicating accurately and honestly and thereby providing many development opportunities for board members via the simple act of communication—either verbal or written.

Richard Maurer; Pearl River I have had two experiences in this regard. In Pearl River, the school board members were for the most part the same members who were present when the district won the New York State Governor's Award. This is a state award modeled in many aspects to the Baldrige Criteria. They had experienced the tremendous public relations gain the district had achieved in the county and local community when the award was announced. Home property values increased as parents sought to move into Pearl River because of the perceived value of the school system. Local private and parochial schools had students leave to register in the public Pearl River School District. In New York State the school district budget is voted on by members of the community every May for the following school year. The school board saw the percentage of positive yes votes increase dramatically for many years after the Governor's award was presented. Therefore, for members of the Pearl River school board, they saw the opportunity to be awarded a national award as increasing the perceived value of the school district to the community. I remember presenting the Baldrige process at a special board workshop where the board asked many questions about the process. They saw the process as fitting into the continuous improvement philosophy that the district already had. In fact, Pearl River had participated in the Baldrige education pilot award process in the early 1990s, so there was a comfortable feeling about the process.

In Ardsley, the school board members did not have much knowledge of the award. I remember at my interview sessions with them prior to being offered the job, I asked if they would be interested in the district working toward achieving the Baldrige Award. I remember distinctly they said they knew little of it but that it was not a goal. As I began to implement the process in the district, not as Baldrige but as a continuous improvement model, they became familiar with the terms and began to see value in the processes. For example, the idea of surveying the stakeholders to discover their perceptions of the district impressed them. In addition, the focus on strategic planning provided them with clear objectives focused on need. They began to view the Baldrige process as a way to bring a different kind of model, a business model, into the district. Their perceived value for the Baldrige process is in obtaining critical feedback to improve the organization. The award itself, at this writing, is not an important goal. The improvement process, however, has allowed them the buy-in.

John Conyers; District 15 I was fortunate in that I had been in the district for many years. A level of trust between the administration and the board of education had been painstakingly built. Board members cannot be expected just to buy into a concept like Baldrige unless you have previously developed a strong base of support and trust. This doesn't happen overnight, but rather is a relationship evolved over the years by running a quality school system. Board of education members must believe that the information they are receiving is the unvarnished truth, and it's probably best to err on the side of giving them too much information. A positive relationship with the entire board begins with gaining the trust of each individual member. Some may refer to this as "the care and feeding of board members." I prefer to consider it simply building trust in the organization.

To attain buy-in for the Baldrige process, I began by talking to each board member about how we could become more accountable to our customers by using a data-based decision approach. I stressed the need to align all district systems so they as a board could hold me more accountable as a superintendent, using data to achieve true apples-to-apples accountability. I led them to the understanding that no organization can be successful without being aligned to a strategic plan . . . to a district vision . . . to district goals . . . and to performance standards. I gave them questions dealing with alignment, the focus of the organization, data analysis, and results—the very things that they should be holding me accountable for.

I began by talking to each board member about how we could become more accountable to our customers by using a data-based decision approach. I stressed the need to align all district systems so they as a board could hold me more accountable as a superintendent.

Now I was ready to start pushing the flywheel and getting more fingerprints on the issue of the Malcolm Baldrige Criteria. I also began sharing my conviction that there were no excuses for getting the kind of results that we were getting, and that we were perfectly aligned to those negative results. I told them that we could do better with *all* 13,000 of our students. Of course, some were doing well, but when we disaggregated results by minority strata and socioeconomic strata, it was apparent we were letting many kids fall through the cracks. In fact, I asked the board, "Could our detractors be correct in saying that we are not making a real difference in what these students achieve?"

During goal development I told the board, "There are no excuses for not using the best internationally recognized standard for measuring organizational excellence to seek outside feedback in order to improve." That, of course, was the Baldrige Criteria. I encouraged the board of education to adopt as its very first priority goal: "To excel as an organization, continually raising the benchmark in all categories of the Baldrige National Quality Award." I recommended that we immediately begin working to achieve the Lincoln Foundation for Business Excellence Award, an Illinois award based on the Baldrige Criteria. Then I sealed the agreement with each board of education member that they would support this approach, holding me accountable throughout the process.

Board of education members want to do a good job—and I was able to show them that by using the Baldrige, they were demonstrating a significantly higher level of accountability to the community. The Baldrige helps keep board focus, aligns the board to take action on the important issues of the district, and moves single-issue candidates to think about broader district issues.

Charles Sorensen; UW-Stout The UW System has a 17-member board of regents for its institutions: 2 doctoral universities, 11 comprehensive universities, and 13 two-year transfer campuses. The System is headed by a president who coordinates the campus chancellors. In this confederated system, each campus is given a great degree of flexibility to manage the campus, guided by board policy; drive the mission of the campus; establish a vision; and position the campus strategically in a highly competitive higher education market. When I announced to System president Katharine Lyall that we intended to apply for the Malcolm Baldrige National Quality Award, she encouraged the campus to do so. The UW System has always been very data driven—collecting, sharing, and making decisions based on data trends and analysis, aligning nicely with the expectations of the Baldrige Criteria. Business executives serving on the board of regents were quite aware of the Baldrige Award, its prestige, the difficulty of actually receiving the award, and the impact it had on companies. Both the System and the board understood that we were an exceptional campus, focused on corporate and business partnerships, very data driven and confident that we could compete with colleges and universities in best practices.

When we received the award in 2001, the System and the board were pleased and proud that a Wisconsin university set the standard for universities nationwide.

Question 3

Who was most critical to get on board with you from the start and why? Did that vary based on where you were in the process?

Answers

Kirby Lehman; Jenks In a school district, it is critically important that middle managers, specifically school principals, get on board early in any improvement initiative. This was definitely true in our district. One method we used was to identify, initiate, and sustain a Continuous Improvement Leadership Team (CILT), with membership including principals from all levels. In short, the principals soon became an integral part of making the true leadership and directional decisions for the entire district. Even though all principals were not directly involved in the CILT, all principals felt (at least indirectly) involved through the involvement of their principal peers.

Richard DeLorenzo; Chugach Everyone wants to make a difference. We need to believe this. We just seem to get lost along the way. Initially, the two most critical stakeholder groups are school boards because they set policy and are the gatekeepers, and teachers because they are in the trenches making it happen each day. School boards want to help schools become better, and teachers want their classrooms to

Initially, the two most critical stakeholder groups are school boards because they set policy and are the gatekeepers, and teachers because they are in the trenches making it happen each day.

be more productive, but rarely do they have the tools and processes to make it happen.

In retrospect, I would have been much more strategic by involving the students from the beginning. This is all about them and their future, and their voice is one we often neglect. With our foundation we have now been much more deliberate with student involvement and have seen much more commitment from all of our stakeholders because of this. Figure 1 depicts the key steps in implementing a performance-based educational system.

John Conyers; District 15 It is my experience that Baldrige works best top down. Then, in high-performing organizations, it bubbles up. At the same time that I was gaining support from the board of education, I began to bring my

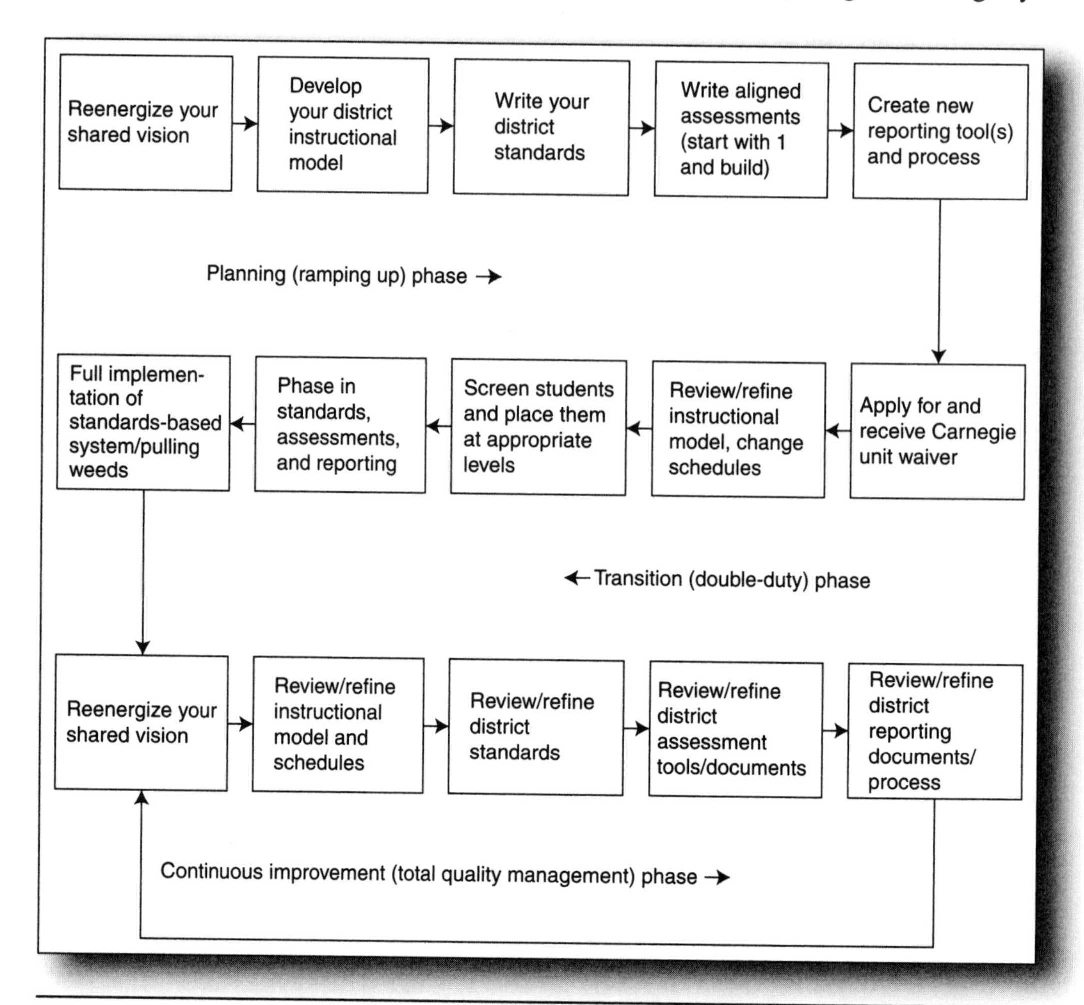

Figure 1 Chugach three phases of implementing a performance-based educational system.

> *It is my experience that Baldrige works best top down. Then, in high-performing organizations, it bubbles up.*

cabinet members to a new level of data-driven decision making and accountability. The old saw "In God we trust, all others bring data" was my line in the sand. I was no longer going to deal with problems brought to me unless I knew that senior leaders in the organization were using PDSA, data analysis, and operational definitions in their departments to analyze and address those problems. This was a big change, and it definitely caused some heated and uncomfortable times in cabinet meetings and individual departmental reviews! Eventually, however, I convinced them all that this new approach, although not traditional in educational organizations, had considerable merit. Now, more hands were on the flywheel (as Jim Collins likes to call it), but I refer to it as getting more fingerprints on the process.

Our district is in a heavily unionized state, and within the district itself there are three unions. It was critical to bring union leaders on board early. I have always believed that to ensure contract approval and union support, you must work at it every single day. Communication channels must be open, and trust must be built with all employees in the organization. I definitely viewed our 2200 employees as internal customers that needed my attention. I knew that we could never secure satisfaction from our end customers (students, parents, and the community) without first meeting the needs of these crucial internal customers. I began by asking: Do we market a product? If so, what is it? Over the next few months, I went to more than 1800 employees in all departments and schools to ask them: If you could change one thing in this district without spending money and naming names, what would it be? Next I asked, What would delight you in this organization? An additional question was asked of teachers and principals: What would happen if we stopped making excuses for our failures to truly have all of our kids meet or exceed state and national standards? Then I shared their responses, posting them on the district intranet for all to see. Although no one had expected me to show to others what my mother used to describe as our "dirty linen," none of that information was ever shared outside the organization. That's a tribute to our wonderful staff and to the internal pride that was building in the organization.

An important caveat for administrators: You cannot just rely on your union organizations to bring your internal customers to the table of accountability. You have to reach out to your employees, show them how this will benefit not only the organization but also each of them personally, and build their trust by making them a willing part of the process.

Joe Alexander; Monfort For us, it was getting our senior faculty and central administration (analogous to our parent company at the university) on board. I outline in a different question how we worked to solidify the commitments of our faculty and staff. Making the case to our central administration that this would be good for the college and the university was not that difficult in 2002, given we had already made the hard choices many years ago of committing to a focused undergraduate mission. I believe the administration saw this as a natural progression from where we had been and consistent with an approach that would build a stronger college which could enhance the overall quality of the university. I do think that demonstrating to them that we were not asking for additional financial resources to support our goal, but merely for the administrative space in which to navigate as we continued using this new framework to improve, was key to maintaining their support.

Charles Sorensen; UW-Stout In response to a 1996 campus crisis questioning leadership decision making, we reorganized our administrative structure so we would be more responsive to campus issues and more inclusive in the decision-making process. Part of the reorganization was the creation of the Chancellor's Advisory Council (CAC), a broad-based group of 20 representing all constituencies on campus. This became the first body, and perhaps the most important, to see the advantage of the award and support the decision. While there was little resistance by CAC members, they did ask tough, penetrating questions that forced us to clarify our reasoning and thereby develop a deeper and more meaningful rationale for applying for the award. Shared governance is strong here, and the three senates—the Faculty Senate, the Senate of Academic Staff (a nontenure category of teaching and administrative staff), and the Stout Student Association—all supported the effort but only after considerable discussion of the Baldrige principles and the evaluation categories. We made a strategic decision not to ask the faculty and teaching academic staff to engage the Baldrige in the classroom, averting an issue that would undoubtedly have derailed our effort; and in the end, governance supported our effort, and several key faculty assisted in the application process.

We maintained an open dialogue with all groups on campus, did a credible job of preparing the campus for the site visit, and invited the entire campus to celebrate when we achieved the distinction of being the first university to be awarded the Baldrige in 2001.

Steve Mittlestet; Richland College It was vital to get every member of Richland's executive leadership team on board at the beginning. We made some false starts and realized we had to be willing to learn together (assisted by Quality Texas examiner training), wrestle with concepts, [and] have robust conversations without diminishing one another (we've gotten better at this). We also learned to pilot approaches prior to full deployment so as not to confuse or dispirit those willing to experiment with us or to deepen cynicism in those who may have considered us hopeless even before we considered launching this journey.

We made some false starts and realized we had to be willing to learn together, wrestle with concepts, [and] have robust conversations without diminishing one another.

Question 4

How do you involve teachers and administrators in Baldrige without overwhelming them and turning them off?

Answers

Kirby Lehman; Jenks Involving teachers and administrators without overwhelming them almost necessitates taking initial steps that are small and understandable for all participants. Ideally, early in any procedural change, teachers and principals would be called on to give presentations in front of their peers—presentations that reflect a "digestible nugget" of the Criteria or whatever other issue or development the district might be addressing or introducing at that time. The first key is to take small steps in the implementation process—steps that all participants have the capacity to fully understand. The second key is to develop ownership, and oftentimes successful ownership is cultivated through staff members' development of presentations on specific issues, especially when done in front of their peers.

The first key is to take small steps in the implementation process—steps that all participants have the capacity to fully understand.

Richard Maurer; Pearl River I always start the Baldrige process with a focus on organizational improvement, not necessarily teacher improvement. I try not to use the term "Baldrige," because it takes too much effort to explain, and most educators will view it as a type of canned curriculum, like a reading or math series. I use the term "continuous improvement" because it describes a process, not content. It is not something you purchase, experiment with, get trained in, and are held accountable for. Baldrige really is a means to align the different processes of an organization around its purpose, mission, and values. Thus it makes sense to start with the administrators first. The teachers can be brought on later and only then with involvement in those areas that they have control over. I will explain two processes that help involve the administrators and one process that involves the teachers. None of them will overwhelm the user. More than likely they will help clarify the continuous improvement process.

I use the term "continuous improvement" because it describes a process, not content. . . . Baldrige really is a means to align the different processes of an organization around its purpose, mission, and values. Thus it makes sense to start with the administrators first.

The first is the golden thread. Figure 2 is a linear diagram of how strategic goals, long-term objectives, and short-term objectives can be aligned. The golden thread eliminates disconnects that can occur between school district planning, assessments, and eventual outcomes.

Administrators like it because it clearly shows how all the varied objectives in a school and a district are connected to one another. It shows the relative importance of each type of objective in terms of supporting the strategic objective. It helps fend off attempts by other stakeholders to add projects, goals, or objectives along the way that do not support the strategic objective. Figure 3 demonstrates how the golden thread can be used to organize improvement on high school English achievement.

Here the strategic goal is to improve academic achievement. The long-term goal, or lag goal, is to improve the English achievement at the high school. The lead goal, or short-term goal, is to improve eighth-grade reading achievement.

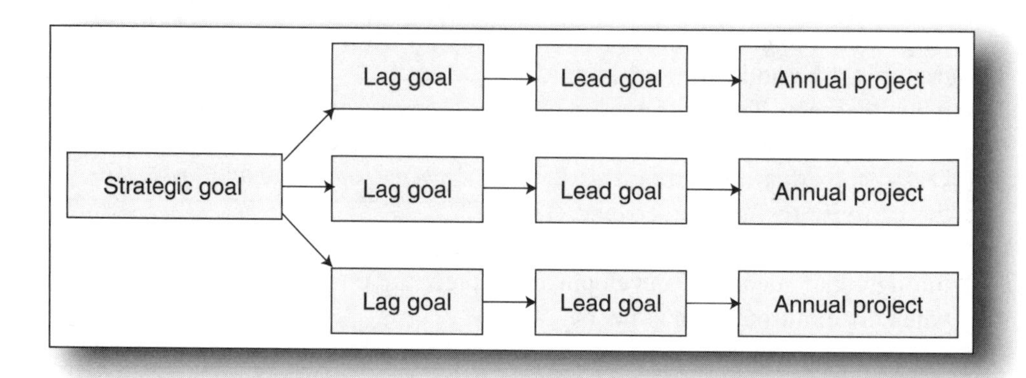

Figure 2 Pearl River golden thread.

Strategic Goal: Academic Achievement		
Lag Goals	**Lead Goals**	**Annual Project**
High school English passing rate	Eighth-grade reading proficiency rate	Implement teaching unit on how to infer meaning of a story

Figure 3 Pearl River applying the golden thread.

The logic is that if students can perform well in reading as they exit eighth grade, their chances of succeeding in high school, specifically high school English, raises significantly. Another short-term goal is to improve the fourth-grade reading achievement. The same logic would apply here toward student success in middle or junior high school.

The second process that is helpful to introduce Baldrige is to require administrators to submit quarterly reports on their progress toward achieving the strategic goals. The format of this report is critical to aligning the action plans to the successful attainment of the goal. I use a format that follows the process of plan, deploy, results. For each of the short-term goals, I require the administrator to write a plan to attain the results desired. Next he or she needs to list the deployment or implementation strategies that will be undertaken to implement the plan. Lastly I expect the results section to describe what occurred. It is expected that if the plan and the deployment strategies are aligned, the result desired will be achieved. If the results are not achieved, then there is a flaw in the plan or the deployment strategy. In either case, the administrator needs to review the plan and/or deployment strategies to determine where the disconnect is located.

By requiring the quarterly report, it is possible to get a quick assessment of progress and to intervene where possible to correct evident disconnects. This report also serves to make the administrator cognitively aware that there is a process of plan, deploy, results for each goal and secondly that he or she is accountable. The nice part of this format is that it addresses two major weaknesses in most educational goal setting. One is that we spend a huge amount of time developing plans but provide few resources to deploy strategies to make the plans operational. The second is the tendency to dive into action without a plan, thus supporting the dictum that "it does not matter which road you take because you won't know when you arrive." Action without a plan is like throwing the dice hoping that something will materialize and whatever it is declare that it is the result you were reaching for. Figure 4 shows a sample of a fourth-quarter report using the format described. Usually in the first or second quarter there are few results to report since the deployment strategies are just being implemented.

The third process is aimed at helping the teaching staff understand the continuous improvement process. My experience in describing the process to teachers produces an almost immediate validation of what they are already doing. It produces a sort of, "Aah! That is what I have been doing all these years." Figure 5

Plan	Deployment strategies	Results
To establish four PC computers in each fourth-grade classroom	Teacher training Student training Software acquisition Establish student technology outcomes	As of June, each fourth-grade student has produced a Microsoft Word document, done research on the Internet, used Microsoft Excel to build graphs, and completed a curriculum PowerPoint presentation.

Figure 4 Pearl River fourth-quarter report.

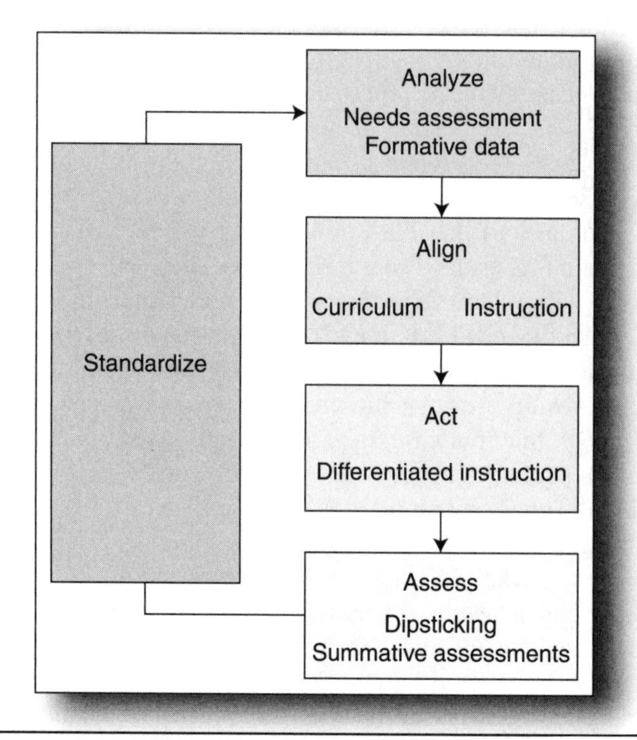

Figure 5 Pearl River A+ approach.

shows the A+ process that describes the process that teachers use to help all students in their classes achieve an A+ or the highest level of achievement they are capable of achieving.

The process begins with assessing at what level is student performance. There is an analysis of the data to determine what is expected and what was obtained. The teacher has two areas to address to close the gap. The first may be aligning the curriculum or the "what" that was taught. Use of a curriculum map is helpful here to benchmark local curriculum to that of the state or national standard. The other area is to change instruction. Here the teacher may want to introduce more differentiation or more technology infused into the classroom work. The next task of the teacher is to assess student performance to determine whether one or both of the strategies deployed have closed the gap. If they have, then the process is standardized. If the gap still remains wide, then the plan needs to be revised.

In any case, the A+ approach demonstrates to the teacher that a continuous improvement process can be deployed to improve student performance.

John Conyers; District 15 First of all, do not "Baldrige" everybody at once. Teachers will push back with, "You want me to do what?" Start at the top, model the Criteria, then begin by working with a few teachers who volunteer to pioneer quality tools, data analysis, and data-driven teaching strategies. Their successes will start a chain reaction that spreads to other teachers and even percolates down to students and their parents quickly—because it works!

> *Do not "Baldrige" everybody at once. Teachers will push back with, "You want me to do what?" Start at the top, model the Criteria, then begin by working with a few teachers who volunteer to pioneer quality tools, data analysis, and data-driven teaching strategies.*

Second, do not waste time with the resisters and blockers in your organization. Watch out for the 90/10 rule: do not spend 90 percent of your time trying to convert the 10 percent of resisters. So empower those who embrace the process and work the undecided in your organization, but don't waste time or agonize over those you can't convince.

Third, stay close to your unions. "Dipstick" your organization often by constantly talking to your employees or internal customers. Then get your early celebrations in front of the board of education and even the public as often as you can so people start seeing that things really *are* different in your organization.

Fourth, share information. We established a policy that said: "There are no excuses for not giving the right information to the right people at the right time." Giving people the tools to mine data within the organization improves the culture as well as the performance. Eventually we were able to track more than 200 quality variables through our data warehouse. Now that's data-driven decision making!

> *We established a policy that said: "There are no excuses for not giving the right information to the right people at the right time."*

Charles Sorensen; UW-Stout At UW-Stout, the Baldrige Criteria and process are primarily used by senior leaders in the management of the institution and in the alignment and integration of key processes and data into a system for education. Faculty members are involved in Baldrige efforts through their participation in governance groups, task forces, and campus-wide committees as well as their involvement in core processes such as strategic planning, new curriculum development, or program review. Although training in the Baldrige values, categories, Criteria, and quality tools is made available to the campus, this training is not extensive or mandatory. There is no campus-wide attempt to integrate Baldrige or other quality tools in the classroom.

The campus has been successful in integrating the Baldrige Criteria into the daily operation and management of the institution rather than promoting Baldrige as a special quality improvement initiative with many new teams and improvement projects. Instead, improvement projects, as identified through Baldrige feedback or as part of the annual planning process, are most often assigned to existing offices, governance groups, or committees. Individuals involved in improvement projects are encouraged to seek out best practices, review existing data, and, if necessary, collect additional data to make informed decisions on which to base their recommendations.

When the Baldrige site visits occurred, the examining team did not find a campus full of Baldrige experts but rather faculty and staff who were committed to the mission, values, and goals of UW-Stout. There was an environment of shared leadership, trust, and open communication. The faculty and staff interviewed by the examiners were able to articulate their relationships with students and stakeholder groups, their roles in key processes, and the types of data and information they access and use to make decisions regarding their work, both in and out of the classroom.

UW-Stout provides numerous training and professional development opportunities to new and continuing employees, including introductory Baldrige training and leadership development programs. Faculty and staff also gain additional knowledge and experience with the Baldrige Criteria as they move into various roles on campus, such as program director, department chair, or governance leader. However, over the years, it has become simply the way we do business at UW-Stout, and faculty and staff have recognized the value in implementing the Baldrige Criteria and take pride in UW-Stout's reputation as a leader in this area. The Baldrige model, for us, now provides a framework and set of criteria for common understanding and communication within the university, and alignment of organization imperatives.

Question 5

Everyone wants a road map to implementing Baldrige. They want to know what steps to take when. What was your road map? Were you certain about it before you started, or did you make it up as you went? Why? If you were starting over, would it look the same?

Answers

Kirby Lehman; Jenks Although there is no easy road map to implementing Baldrige in any institution, in our school district we developed the Framework for Quality and stuck to it. It has served as a framework for goal setting, the development of strategic objectives, and for the development of action plans for striving to reach our goals. Figure 6 depicts our Framework for Quality, and Figure 7 shows how we move from our vision, mission, and values to action.

Although there is no easy road map to implementing Baldrige in any institution, in our school district we developed the Framework for Quality and stuck to it.

Richard Maurer; Pearl River A school district should start with the Organizational Profile in the Baldrige application. This requires the district to think about defining its main educational programs, offerings, and services. In addition, the purpose, vision, mission, and values are defined and articulated. The district has to gather some

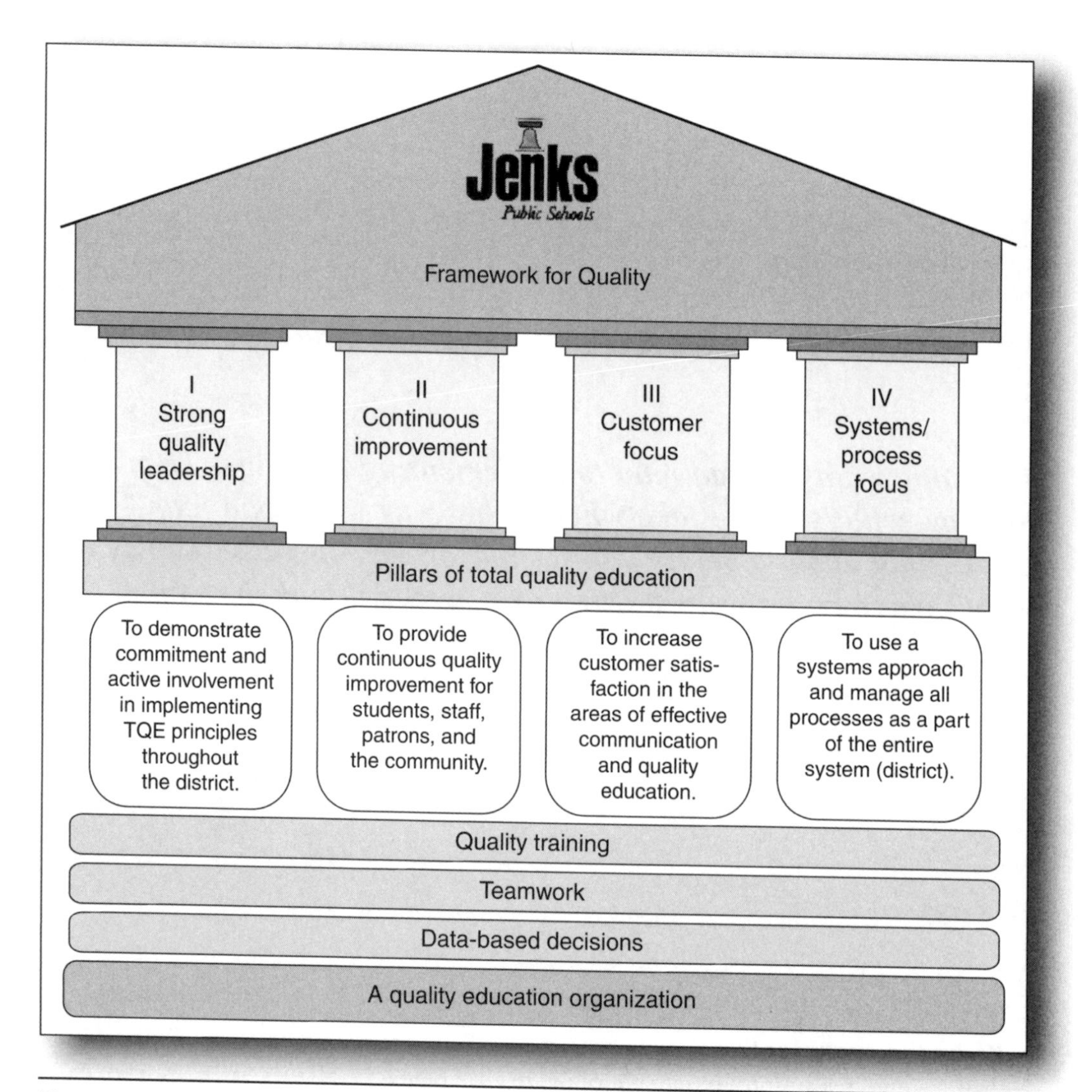

Figure 6 Jenks Framework for Quality.

data on its faculty and staff and workforce diversity. A big area to define is the regulatory environment under which the district operates. The profile requires a district to determine who its stakeholder is, its markets, suppliers, and partners. The relationship of all of these to the district needs to be defined. Another big piece is defining the competitive environment such as what other school districts serve as benchmarks to the district and where do comparative data come from. The key education and learning challenges, human resources, and performance improvement systems are defined.

Start with the Organizational Profile in the Baldrige application. This requires the district to think about defining its main educational programs, offerings, and services.

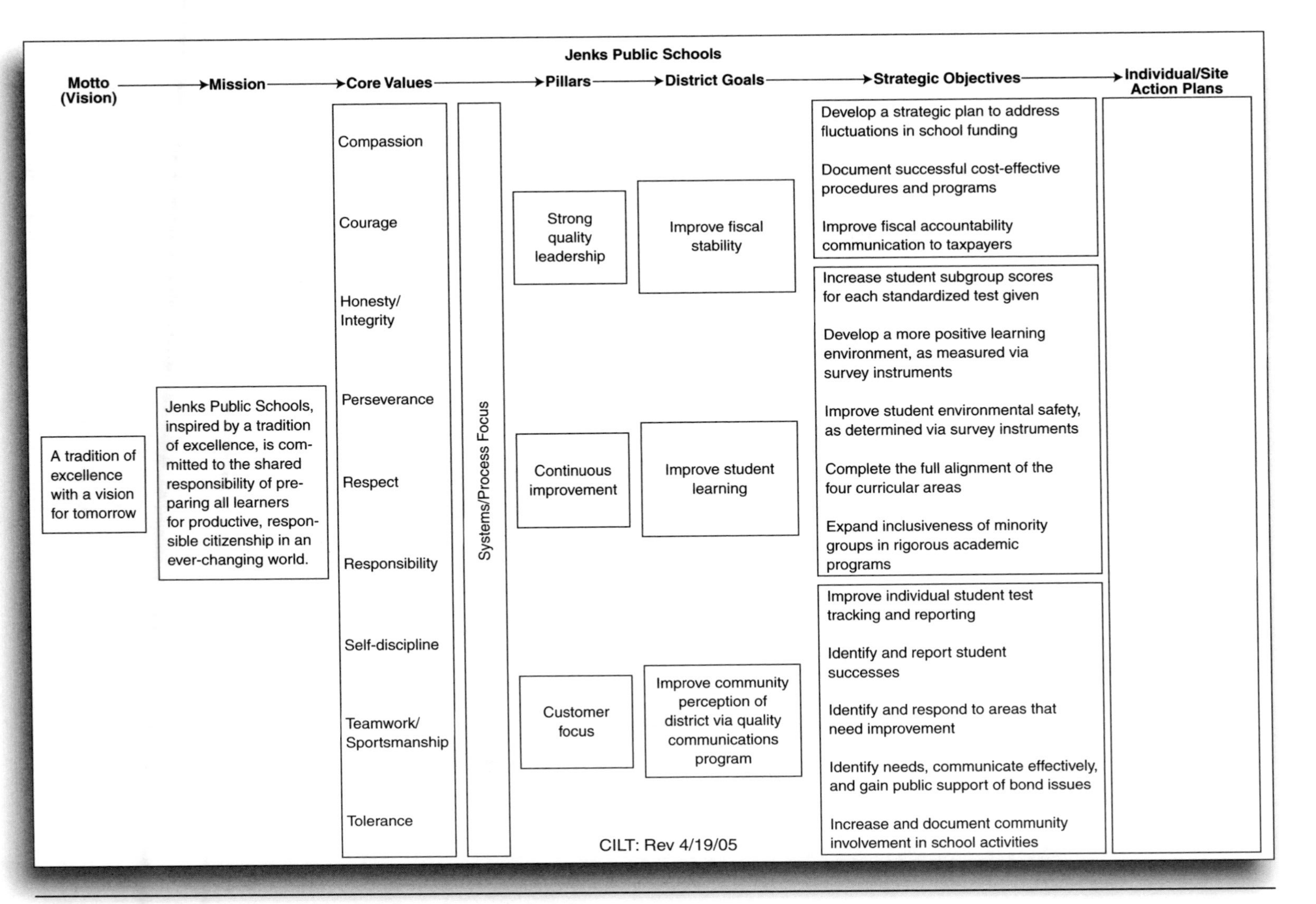

Figure 7 Jenks Public Schools: Vision, mission, values to action plans.

I have found that completing this profile is key to driving improvement. It defines where the district is now. When we first read the questions in the profile, we thought they would be easy to answer. They were not. It took hours of discussion and debate among the administrative team.

The next step on the road map is to go back to one of the questions in the profile. Who are the stakeholders and how are their needs assessed is one such question. The district should devise a number of survey instruments for parents, students, and staff. I would recommend using a commercial product such as provided by Harris Interactive from Rochester, New York. The data analysis the firm provides is valuable in defining the key needs of the various stakeholders. This information will provide the basis to answering information in Category 3, "Student, Stakeholder, and Market Focus."

The next step is to look at Category 7.1, "Student Learning Outcomes." Most districts have achievement data stored in some form of electronic warehouse, and most have already completed analysis of curriculum and/or grade level areas that need areas of improvement. Collecting the academic data and displaying them in a graph format make them easy to understand. A discussion among faculty and staff should take place about what areas identified should be prioritized. It is my experience that to focus on improvement in all those areas identified will result in frustration. The expenditure of resources will exhaust any efforts to make improvement across all areas.

So up to this step in the road map, the profile is completed, data are gathered on stakeholder satisfaction, and data have been collected in those academic areas chosen to need improvement.

The next phase is to develop a strategic plan or to focus on the objectives outlined in Category 2. The first part of the focus should be a discussion about how the team is going to develop its plan: What are the key steps to take, and who in the district needs to be brought on board. A team should begin the process of deciding what key objectives are to be placed in the plan. One area to start is to take the lowest areas of reported satisfaction on the various survey instruments and choose them as key objectives. Some of the lowest areas may not be ones a district would want to focus on, but the discussion would decide the key ones. A similar process should take place for key academic data. At this point, the beginnings of a strategic plan can take place. The format shown in Figure 8 is a useful guide.

The next part of the road map is to determine how the strategic plan is going to be deployed throughout the district. Here, action plans are developed with a familiar format of who is doing what and when. To complete a meaningful deployment strategy, the team will have to focus on a number of other key areas. "Faculty and Staff Focus" issues, as outlined in Category 5, and "Process Measurement," as outlined in Category 6, will provide insight on how these two areas can support deployment of the plan. Of course, the management of the data needs to take place, and Category 4, "Measurement, Analysis, and Knowledge Management," will guide a team through methods to manage this task.

Goal	Performance	Starting Point (year)	Midpoint (year)	Long-Term Goal (year)
Improve reading	Percentage of third graders achieving a 4 on a state exam based on a scale of 1 to 4.	77%	85%	95%
Improve student satisfaction in technology	Percentage reporting positive on annual survey	50%	60%	80%

Figure 8 Pearl River guide for strategic planning.

The road map is not complete, but the team has in place the basic building blocks to start addressing the Criteria in the Baldrige application.

John Conyers; District 15 If leading an organization were easy, most organizations would be excellent. Although adopting the Baldrige was sometimes a tough sell, I recognized that it was incumbent on me as the district's leader to inspire a change for the better. Several factors convinced me that the Baldrige approach was the correct strategy:

- The Baldrige has a long history of helping organizations move from good to great.
- The Baldrige Criteria are an integration of leading-edge organizational practices derived from many sources that have been improved over the past 18 years.
- The Criteria are a validated model of how to manage an organization and an internationally recognized benchmark of organizational excellence.
- It defines a set of core values for performance excellence.
- It can be used to help manage an organization.
- It is a powerful self-assessment tool.
- It helps organizations build capacity to accelerate and sustain continuous improvement.
- It provides a framework for driving excellence through organizations already perceived to be high performing.

Personally, it fulfilled another of my requirements—to silence critics from the private sector who say that we educators are only interested in test scores and lagging indicators. Educators and educational organizations clearly can achieve the same levels of organizational improvement that are usually attributed only to business organizations. District 15 did, and the 2003 Malcolm Baldrige Award acknowledged our success.

Following the Baldrige Criteria would be hard to do on the fly. You can't just make it up as you go along, because the performance indicator questions are so finite, clear, and accountable. We integrated it into our leadership team (central office senior leaders and building principals) through the Organizational Effectiveness Cycle developed by the Franklin Covey Company, and we enhanced it by overlaying the Baldrige Criteria at the appropriate steps to further refine the self-assessment approach within the cycle. Figure 9 aligns the Baldrige categories with the Covey Organizational Effectiveness Cycle.

Our road map was making effective use of the feedback report from our applications for the state quality award presented by the Lincoln Foundation for Business Excellence. It took two tries, but we were able to achieve the highest award possible from the Lincoln Foundation. The feedback reports were a

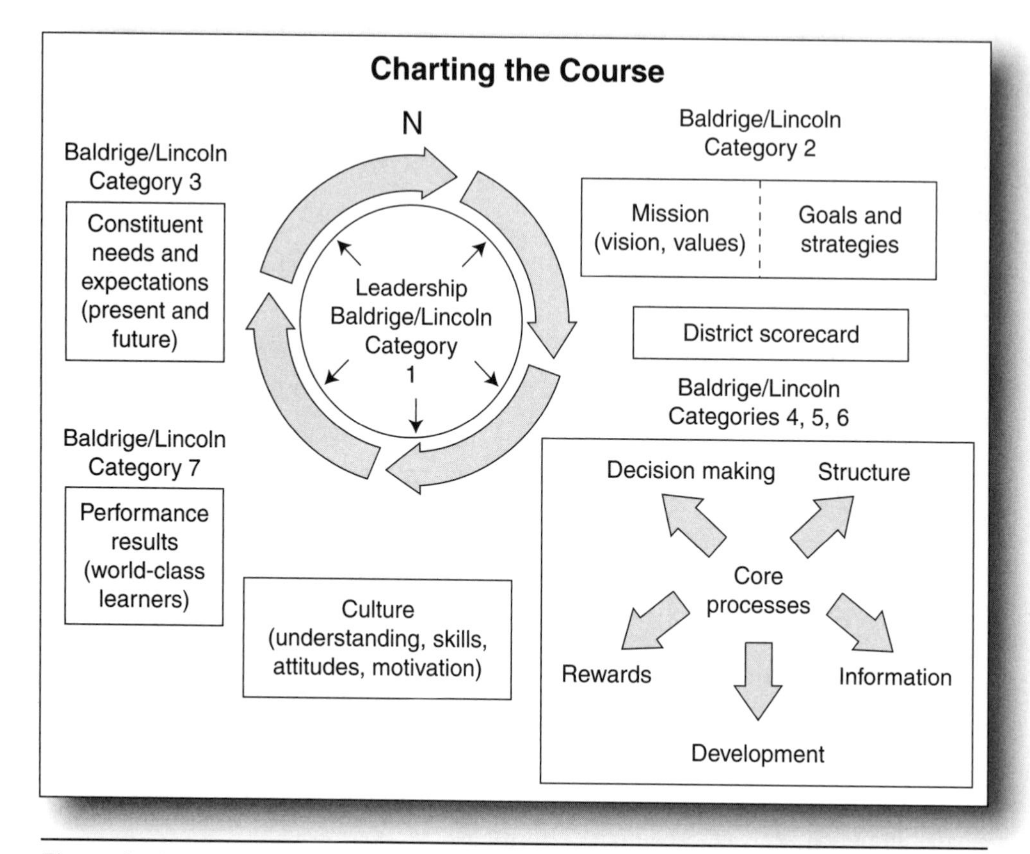

Figure 9 Baldrige/Covey crosswalk.

Source: John G. Conyers and Robert Ewy, *Charting Your Course: Lessons Learned During the Journey Toward Performance Excellence* (Milwaukee, WI: ASQ Quality Press, 2004), 84, 85. Used with permission of Conyers JJ & Associates/Robert Ewy.

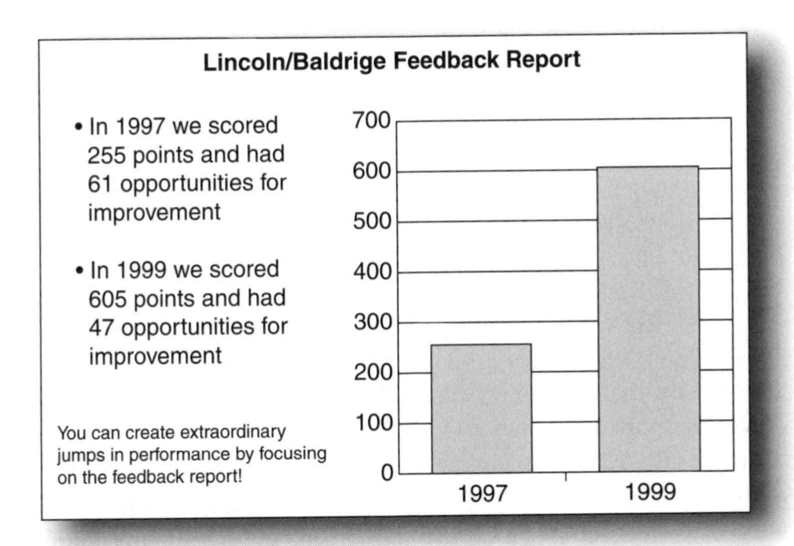

Figure 10 District 15 Lincoln feedback gains.

Source: Conyers JJ & Associates/Robert Ewy

tremendous help in knowing which areas to address, as was the feedback report from the site visit we earned in our first application for the Baldrige Award. Based on my experience working with private sector consulting firms, I now know that these feedback reports could be worth as much as $75,000 in consulting fees—making the minimal Lincoln and Baldrige application fees an excellent investment. Figure 10 shows the improvement in feedback scores from 1997 to 1999.

After achieving the state award, we celebrated, an important milestone on any road map toward performance excellence. With the Lincoln Award in hand, we immediately targeted the Malcolm Baldrige National Quality Award. An initial step was directing all school district administrators to become state or national quality examiners. Some were to become skilled in Six Sigma, others to become Lincoln Foundation examiners.

If we were to prepare a road map for Baldrige implementation based on our experience, it might look like this:

1. Lead. Just do it. Start talking about quality, ask questions, raise the bar, let people know there are no acceptable excuses for poor performance.
2. Build trust in the organization. A positive culture is everything, and it is the hardest to attain and maintain. Remember, the longer people are in the organization, the more like the organization they become, so work hard on positive culture.
3. Align the system.
4. Measure the system.

5. Make decisions based on your measurements.

6. Focus on results, because if American public education is to survive, we must see better results.

7. Find benchmarks anywhere you can. Start with APQC [American Productivity and Quality Center]. Only with the benchmarking process will you really get *breakthrough* improvement.

8. Celebrate whenever you can! Celebrate all your wins, large or small.

We always said that implementing the Baldrige Criteria was not about winning an award. Of course, we were gratified when we did, but there were many more important results. Over the course of our journey, we built up a lot of trust in the organization, we became more data driven, our quality indicators rose, our departments were aligned and focused on the most important performance indicators, and people were proud to be part of an organization that was receiving positive support from the community for its quality efforts.

Richard DeLorenzo; Chugach I believe our success in the Chugach School District, and later illustrated by the RISC [ReInventing Schools Coalition] Foundation, was based on our ability to simplify the Baldrige concepts into a clear road map with functional processes. We have synthesized the Baldrige seven categories into four components: *Leadership, Shared Vision, Standards-Based Design,* and *Continuous Improvement.* These four components have had the greatest impact on creating a new paradigm in our schools without being bogged down with ambiguous Baldrige terminology. It is vital for any organization that deploys this quality journey to simplify the concepts being addressed and include *all* key stakeholders along the way. If we want quality schools, we need to move toward a cultural change where the next generation has the knowledge and skills to carry the torch of hope for our children. If we lose them in the early restructuring stages, our chances of carrying the vision forward are greatly diminished.

We have synthesized the Baldrige seven categories into four components: Leadership, Shared Vision, Standards-Based Design, and Continuous Improvement.

It is vital for any organization that deploys this quality journey to simplify the concepts being addressed and include all key stakeholders along the way.

This means making difficult decisions, changing policy, increasing student contact days, lobbying state and national policy makers, even replacing Carnegie units with graduation by performance levels. Many of these changes will not be popular but will honor the vision shared by the majority of stakeholders. Our success as a district can be attributed to the fact that we could prioritize where we needed to go and clearly map out the processes for getting there. We had three phases to help us with that accomplishment. We needed not only to teach the right things to our students, but, just as important, we needed to change our obsolete credit system into a research-based performance system. What we wanted for students was the easy part, but the "how" was the real challenge. We often referred to ourselves as moving from the cutting edge into the bleeding edge of educational reform. When we benchmarked this endeavor, we could not find another system, public or private, that had gone down this road even though the research clearly supported these innovations.

Joe Alexander; Monfort Without meaning to sound trite, I believe the first step in developing and pursuing such a journey is to define and reach consensus on your mission, vision, and values as an organization—just as stated in the Baldrige Criteria. Some individuals have mistakenly characterized our Monfort College of Business journey as a short-term one in that we received the Baldrige Award following only our second formal application. What those individuals failed to realize is that the only way that was possible was because we had already gone through a long-term process and 18 years' worth of refinements in defining a focused identity and mission for our organization.

For us, the Baldrige framework simply worked to boost the octane of our engine and align our efforts to where our various parts were working better together at any given point in time—much like the metaphor of an engine running on all cylinders.

By the time we began formally implementing Baldrige in 2002, what in my mind were the toughest steps on the journey had already been taken. We had determined a direction (i.e., a focus on building excellence in undergraduate business education), and we had selected the vehicle for carrying us forward (i.e., our program strategy of "high-touch, wide-tech, and professional depth").

For us, the Baldrige framework simply worked to boost the octane of our engine and align our efforts to where our various parts were working better together at any given point in time—much like the metaphor of an engine running on all cylinders.

As to whether we were certain about all the steps to be taken when we started, I think the obvious answer was no. What we were sure of was that we were going to write a formal application and use the process to improve our business program. As for how to get started, it's like my friend Dale Crownover, CEO of Texas Nameplate, has been heard to say, "All you have to do is simply read the stated questions in the Baldrige Criteria and begin answering them. It's not rocket science."

In retrospect, that is essentially what we did in beginning our formal implementation. We read each question and began thinking how we would answer them in describing our organization. Some questions we understood better than others, and in some cases, we simply did not have any good answers.

Over the subsequent months and completion of our first 50-page application, even before any formal feedback from the examiners, we had all the opportunities for improvement we could possibly work on staring right back at us from that simple process of reading and answering questions.

The majority of other applicants I have listened to rave about the value of having formal feedback from the experts, and that information was certainly valuable to us as well. But never underestimate the value of a critical self-assessment. For our organization, we derived just as much value from sweating through how to answer those questions and how to apply the concepts to our respective areas. To me, that was our version of working to emerge from the proverbial cocoon and becoming stronger as a result of those exercises.

From there, the rest of our implementation journey was fairly straightforward. Subsequent milestones on the road map were revealed as we interpreted and acted on our external feedback, as well as our internal assessments and analysis.

Charles Sorensen; UW-Stout There isn't a standard one-size-fits-all approach to implementing the Baldrige Criteria in an educational institution. A number of factors must be considered, including the size, administrative and governance structure, degree of centralization, administrative sophistication, and culture of an institution. The University of Wisconsin-Stout had implemented several major improvements in leadership, planning, budgeting, and technology management prior to formally adopting the Baldrige Criteria and hence was able to baseline its current level of performance against the Baldrige model. Once the senior leadership team was introduced to the Baldrige values and Criteria in 1999, the first step was to conduct a high-level organizational self-assessment using the Criteria. This exercise was facilitated by a senior Baldrige examiner. During this assessment, the team outlined approaches, deployment, and results in each of the categories. The facilitator encouraged the team to identify both role model strengths as well as gaps in each of the categories.

There isn't a standard one-size-fits-all approach to implementing the Baldrige Criteria in an educational institution.

This self-assessment led to two initiatives:

1. The submission of UW-Stout's first Baldrige application a few months later, and

2. The identification of gaps in performance, and the availability and structure of key data and information needed to be addressed both short term and long term.

Although many institutions use the Criteria internally for several years before applying for a state or national quality award, UW-Stout's senior management team believed it was important to prepare and submit an application in order to receive external feedback needed to take the organization to the next level. Although the campus was aware of the application submission, during that first year few individuals outside the senior leadership team received extensive training on the Baldrige Criteria—essentially, it was a top-down initiative.

The first feedback report led UW-Stout toward the next steps in implementation. The senior leadership team, as well as members of campus governance groups and committees, worked systematically to address the many opportunities for improvement outlined in the report. Several processes were formalized, including the complaint management process, and the campus researched and identified additional sources of comparative and benchmark data at the regional and national levels. This led to the formation of a national peer group of universities based on similar missions and/or academic programs, and greater use of nationally normed instruments to measure student learning and satisfaction and to set stretch goals and targets for improvement.

UW-Stout utilizes the sources of comparative and benchmark data outlined in Figure 11.

Faculty, staff, and students were made aware of the Baldrige categories and Criteria at various information and training sessions led by members of the senior leadership team, and the level of intensity heightened as the campus submitted its second application and prepared for its first Baldrige site visit.

Opportunities for improvement from the second feedback report were shared with the senior leadership team, faculty, and staff and integrated into the campus planning process. The vast majority of improvement projects were assigned to members of the senior leadership team or to existing governance groups or committees. UW-Stout created very few additional committees or teams as part of the Baldrige process and hired no new employees to manage the process. Success was derived by integrating this effort into the fabric of the university, not as an add-on activity. As time progressed, Baldrige training efforts continued and several staff members became trained as Baldrige examiners. The level of activity and rate of improvement continued to increase through submission of the third application and second site visit prior to receiving the award late that year.

Today, the journey continues. Each spring, the Office of Budget, Planning, and Analysis provides the senior leadership team with enrollment data, financial data, survey data, and other internal and external reports on student learning, stakeholder satisfaction, and organizational effectiveness. The data are reviewed in detail by the team, and improvement opportunities are identified as part of the university's annual planning and priority identification process. Improvement projects are assigned to senior administrators or existing groups on campus, and progress is monitored every six months. Key steps in this cycle are depicted in Figure 12.

Peers	Mission-similar universities, nationally known universities with similar programs, groups of like universities identified by survey agencies
Best Practices	Institutions identified as "best"
National	All survey/database participants, national averages
Competitors	UW System and UW comprehensive comparisons to establish leadership in our primary market

Figure 11 UW-Stout comparative data sources.

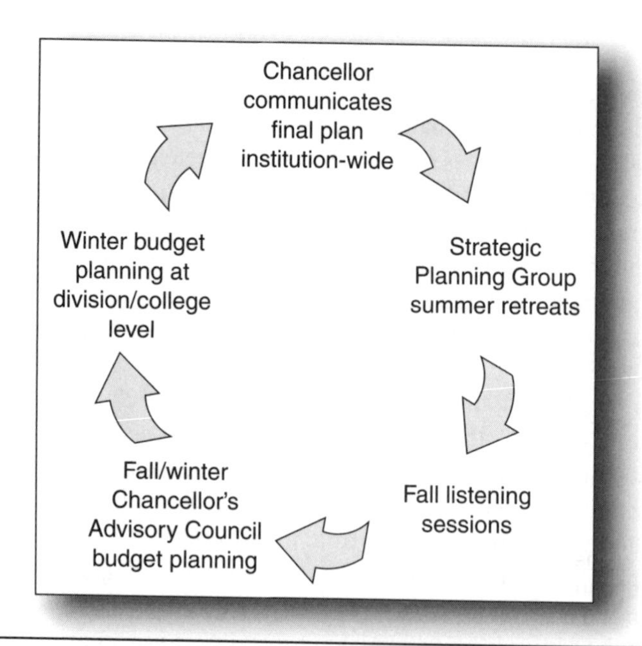

Figure 12 UW-Stout priority planning and development process.

In summary, although there isn't one "right" way to implement the Baldrige Criteria in an educational institution, the UW-Stout approach was to begin with a self-assessment and early submission of a Baldrige application. UW-Stout used the feedback report each year as the basis for making significant improvements, and the university continues to use feedback from internal and external sources as part of the annual planning and priority identification process. This approach has led UW-Stout to become a national leader in quality improvement and demonstrates that universities can change and improve rapidly to meet the needs of students, employers, and society.

Steve Mittlestet; Richland College In the beginning stages of our quality journey, we had no reliable road map. At best we had a compass to keep us moving in the direction of responding to what became our questions we asked ourselves: How do you/others know that your students are learning what you set out for them to learn? How do you know to what extent their learning has served them well and our local and world communities as well, as together we strive to achieve the lofty vision of building a sustainable community for all, now and in the future?

In the beginning stages of our quality journey, we had no reliable road map. At best we had a compass to keep us moving in the direction of responding to what became our questions we asked ourselves.

The Baldrige category questions, especially when they were converted to educational applications, helped us develop appropriate short-term road maps along the way. The questions served as the wise Socratic teacher who knew—by relentlessly, yet supportively asking us the questions—we could find our own wisdom in coming up with systems, processes, programs, and accountability measures that would support us all toward achieving our vision for our students and the communities we serve.

Figure 13 indicates the types of information we sought to understand if we were responding to our core questions, including other higher education institutions as well as Baldrige-winning organizations outside of higher education.

Comparative Information

Inside Higher Education:

- Student and employee surveys
- Peers and competitor colleges
- State agencies for best performers
- Transfer school performance for RLC students
- Sharing groups such as the NCCBP
- Financial comparative performance ratings (e.g., Moody and Fitch)

Outside Higher Education:

Organization	Nature of Benchmark Activity
Ritz-Carlton	*ThunderValue*-of-the-Week
Texas Nameplate	Dashboard
Bank One	Customer service "Front Counter"
Walt Disney Company	Interview/screening, orientation
Starbucks & the "Experience Music Project"	Experience Engineering for T-duck Hall & Future Buildings
Southwest, Container Store	Employee culture
Branch-Smith Printing	Supplier/partner score card
Presbyterian Hospital of Dallas	Employee professional development
Saint Luke's Hospital	Performance Excellence Model

Figure 13 Richland College benchmarks.

Starting over now, we, and others, could speed up the process because we have been influential, as they have been with us, in our journey and in the performance excellence journeys of numerous other higher education entities through such national organizations as the Continuous Quality Improvement Network, League for Innovation in the Community College, Johnson County Community College National Benchmarking Project, and National Community College Survey of Student Engagement—the latter two of which did not exist back in 1997 when we filed Richland's first Texas Level II Assessment application. In other words, the experience of numerous organizations now can be readily accessed and benchmarked to help other organizations avoid starting from scratch, as we had to do in many respects when we began.

Question 6

What do I do with a staff member or board member who is trying to negate the Baldrige implementation process in my district?

Answers

Kirby Lehman; Jenks Working with recalcitrant staff members is part of running a school district. Our experience generally falls into one of two categories. First, involve the staff member in question as deeply as possible in an area where he/she can be an open critic, a presenter, or have direct access to someone that he/she perceives is a decision maker. In short, bring the critic out in the open. Institutional politics would suggest that critics love to be in the background or completely anonymous, except in their own small peer groups. In short, offer such critics the opportunity to have a place at the table and become an *open* critic or participant. Our experiences are that, when given these two choices, staff members oftentimes choose to be positive and contributing participants. Second, recognize that some (hopefully, a small number in any institution) staff members will choose *not* to participate and will choose to remain negative, sniping from the background. However, in well-functioning institutions, when those snipers are given the opportunity to come out in the open and offer positive suggestions, they will often (although not always) do so. If all else fails, and the recalcitrant individual is completing his/her job responsibilities successfully, leadership should not spend an inordinate amount of time attempting to change someone who refuses to change.

Richard Maurer; Pearl River I believe it best to bypass these individuals. In terms of the board member, if you can get the administrators and some key teachers involved and get the process rolling with the understanding that it is continuous improvement, it would be hard for a board member to stop the process. He or she may not like it, but will not try to stop it for fear of causing negative feelings among the staff. I always sold Baldrige as a model to improve organizational performance. This is an area all board members are interested in improving. They usually have little background in curriculum, but they all have organizational background. The idea that a Baldrige application will elicit feedback about the district from experts in the organization/managerial field is an attractive sell point to board members. I always remind them that the application fee is almost nothing compared to bringing in consultants who would cost a significant amount more for the same results. Besides, most board members like to report to their constituents that they have involved the district in a federally sponsored district organization audit.

If a senior administrator is not involved, or worse, trying to negate the process, I have found that the only way to deal with it is up front. I use the Baldrige strategic planning process to set administrators' goals. Usually there are annual projects that support each strategic goal that each administrator must carry out. I require quarterly reports with a focus on results to maintain accountability. It is helpful that administrative salary increases are linked to achievement of annual goals. Not all administrative contracts allow for this, but as a superintendent, I am convinced it is a primary motivator. I have experiences where the administrator is tenured and does not accept the Baldrige process as an area of personal or professional value. In most cases these administrators have felt uncomfortable in their position and in the carrying out of duties. They have left, transferred within the district, or retired. This may seem harsh, but can you imagine in business if a senior vice president or division chief decides that the value of the company and its strategic plan has little value to him or her? He or she would not last long. Why should a school district be any different? If the board and the community set the mission and determine the values of the district, it is the obligation of every administrator to work to align his/her goals to meet these expectations. As administrators we are given a sacred trust by the school community, and we are here to serve, not to dictate our own personal values. If there is a disconnect, it is time to move on.

If you can get the administrators and some key teachers involved and get the process rolling with the understanding that it is continuous improvement, it would be hard for a board member to stop the process.

That being said, I have found in the two districts where I have implemented Baldrige that 99 percent of the administrators have contributed to its success beyond my wildest expectations. I can honestly say that Pearl River would not have been awarded the Baldrige without the involvement of the intelligence, commitment, and creativity of the administrative staff.

John Conyers; District 15 People sometimes become stumbling blocks because they are fearful of change, don't have enough data, or don't feel supported. They may be frightened and sometimes overwhelmed. Perhaps it's just the prospect of what they think will mean more work or working in a different way, or they don't understand what the rewards will be, e.g., "What's in it for me?" Listen carefully and dispassionately to try to understand the negativists. You may actually hear some unpleasant truths—and if that is the case, then move heaven and earth to fix the problems as quickly as possible, within reason. As an administrator and organizational behaviorist, I have found that people block activities in organizations because of their own personal leadership styles. Learn their styles and you will have a window into why they are blockers in your organization and a clue as to how you might be able to bring them on board. We found that after a while our resisters realized they had to come along because parents began driving the Baldrige expectation through their kids' own teachers.

Listen carefully and dispassionately to try to understand the negativists. You may actually hear some unpleasant truths—and if that is the case, then move heaven and earth to fix the problems as quickly as possible, within reason.

Your job as an administrator is to reduce barriers for workers and internal customers so Baldrige work can go on. Check your process data on district activities, check your surveys of staff to identify trouble spots, and then make necessary changes. Do *not* wait for another school year before you correct problems facing staff. Do it immediately, and you will astonish them in a positive way. While all this is going on, do your best to create and maintain a stable environment.

Charles Sorensen; UW-Stout We did have critics on staff who felt that the Baldrige program simply did not fit higher education and that our motive was only to highlight the award itself. We simply answered the critics (and still do) by sharing with them the actual application or the comparative data. We can demonstrate clearly that based on national comparative data, we do extremely well in every category. We also make a point that we had a very difficult time identifying peer schools that were a good match for UW-Stout in such areas as enrollment, program array, and educational philosophy, so we had to search for different peer institutions. Frequently they were division 1 research schools, and they were chosen because of similar programs not found in most state universities. Even in comparison

We simply share data with the critics, and normally this convinces them that the program is appropriate. On more than one occasion, the data we share instill a new sense of pride in the institution.

with these schools, often two or three times the size of UW-Stout, we compared favorably.

In effect, we simply share data with the critics, and normally this convinces them that the program is appropriate. On more than one occasion, the data we share instill a new sense of pride in the institution because whether they assisted directly in the process or not, they played a role in the award by being a contributing member of the university.

Question 7

Some say educators don't understand what a process or a system is. How do you define it for people when you're trying to get them to understand?

Answers

Kirby Lehman; Jenks There is no easy definition of "process" or "system," but we attempt to relate such discussions to our own school system, especially when addressing a systems/process focus, which is part of our Framework for Quality. In short, however, we would attempt to link the concept of continuing development with an orderly arrangement (of issues or things) focused on a logical plan. *Then*, we attempt to relate the above concept with one area of our school district and develop a clear understanding of how that one area relates to and is interdependent with the entire school system.

Richard Maurer; Pearl River The best way is to define it not as theory but as a way to solve a problem. This focus provides the buy-in. For example, both in Pearl River and in Ardsley I have used a consultant who worked for Dell to run workshops on process manage-

The best way is to define it not as theory but as a way to solve a problem. This focus provides the buy-in.

ment. In one example we had difficulty keeping up with the multiple different billing scenarios for out-of-district special-education students. These are students who are classified and are entitled to a variety of services such as one-to-one aides, speech therapy, occupational therapy, counseling, physical therapy, etc., in addition to their tuition costs. The service often changed during the year, and thus the sending district had to have the billing changed if our district was to recoup the cost. It often took months for this change to move from the teacher provider to the principal's office to the special-education office to the business office to the accounts billable department. Our district was losing revenue and creditability with the other districts with the delay in billing and errors. The consultant met with the interested parties, and in two hours they produced a process chart. This is an actual chart of who does what and when with regard to billing of these special-education services. We discovered one accounting procedure changed hands three times, costing us a week and a half of delay. The same process required three sign-offs: the principal, the special-education director, and the business office manager. We reduced the procedure to one sign-off and made it electronic with a critical accounting check later. This saved a week's processing time. The end result was that we reduced real-time billing for special-education services to a three-day process. The increased income the first quarter was between $20,000 and $25,000. The key to our success was that everyone who needed to be involved was part of the solution at this one process-mapping meeting.

The end result was that we reduced real-time billing for special-education services to a three-day process. The increased income the first quarter was between $20,000 and $25,000.

For teachers we have used curriculum mapping as a way to demonstrate system thinking. In Pearl River the third-grade teachers, for example, were located in three separate buildings. To avoid the problem of each building developing curriculum in any one subject, we designed a curriculum mapping process. For social studies, for example, each unit began with an essential question. For example, in studying the American Revolution, a typical essential question might be: Is change good?

For teachers we have used curriculum mapping as a way to demonstrate system thinking.

From this, a series of activities are developed using the format of Plan, Implementation, and Assess for each month of the school year. It can be assumed using the map that all third-grade teachers in the district are incorporating the planned activities each month. The map is not a lockstep method that rigorously binds a teacher to a format. Rather, it is flexible enough to allow the teacher to incorporate some ideas of her own. The main point is that by the end of each month every third grader in the district has completed a core unit using the same activities and the same assessment. Using a curriculum map, there should be no gaps in instruction.

John Conyers; District 15 What educators have not done well so far is to see our districts/schools as systems. Historically, we have not approached improvement from a systems perspective. Clearly, process management and thinking systemically bring major improvement in all areas of the district—but it isn't easy to change old habits. What we did in our district was this:

First, everyone within the organization had to understand that process data are the key. "If it moves, measure it" became our mantra. We started with Webster's definition: "Process—A series of actions or operations conducing to an end," progressed to: "Almost everything an organization does involves a process" (APQC), then went on to: "A process is a systematic series of activities required to achieve a goal" (APQC).

We trained employees to visualize the process through flowcharts and cause-and-effect diagrams. We also trained them to monitor processes through process control charts, histograms, and comparisons.

We trained employees to *visualize* the process through flowcharts and cause-and-effect diagrams. These were the first of the quality tools borrowed from the private sector that all employees quickly learned to use effectively. We also trained them to *monitor* processes through process control charts, histograms, and comparisons.

Figure 14 is an example of how we *visualized* a process, using a flowchart of the School Improvement Planning Process in Consolidated School District 15.

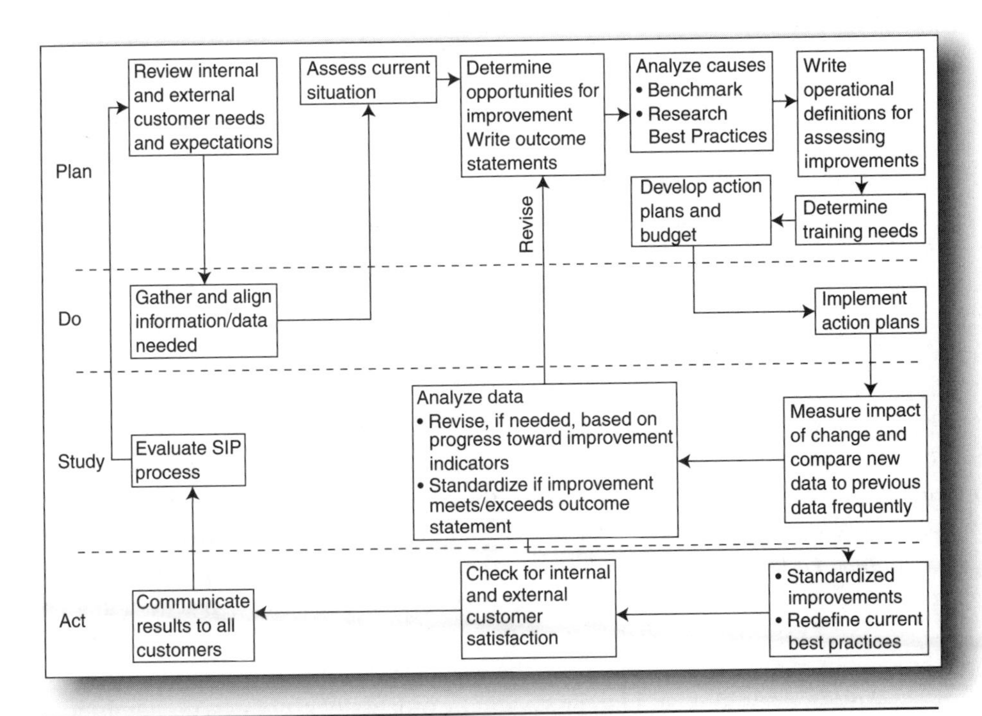

Figure 14 District 15 School Improvement Plan Model.

Source: John G. Conyers and Robert Ewy, *Charting Your Course: Lessons Learned During the Journey Toward Performance Excellence* (Milwaukee, WI: ASQ Quality Press, 2004), 92. Used with permission of Conyers JJ & Associates/Robert Ewy.

Helping teachers understand which processes are working in their assessment results and which ones are not helps them understand the value of process management. We began by asking teachers to identify the most important data they needed to make process improvements. We started with 20 basic questions such as, What are the characteristics of students making the most dramatic standardized test score improvements? We set up a knowledge management system to give teachers easy access to this type of information as well as examples of effective teaching processes, benchmarks, and continuous improvement techniques. It was a very popular internal Web site.

W. Edwards Deming taught us that as much as 94 percent of most of our troubles belongs to the system (or the responsibility of management), and only 6 percent is attributable to other causes. System thinking and process management relax the resisters somewhat because you are no longer searching for the guilty.

Charles Sorensen; UW-Stout This is one of the most difficult things we struggled with as a leadership team in the early stages: to understand a process or systems approach to quality improvement rather than simply relating success stories that seemed to indicate university strengths. Faculty, too, had difficulty understanding that a process is a way of doing things, or a system is a set of interrelated parts that lead to a whole and that one must demonstrate the cause/effect impact of processes or systems on improvement. It is easy and understandable to cite stand-alone data as reflective of quality or strengths. Strong graduation rates or retention rates may reflect quality, but why?

So I use a simple example to explain a process at UW-Stout to show the interdependent relationship of a system. If we are to understand retention or graduation rates, for example, in some meaningful way, then simply citing the data will not work. The graduation rate depends on many variables, beginning with the recruitment of freshmen or transfer students. If a university recruits students with average or poor standardized test scores, high school grades, or class standings, then the probability of high retention rates or graduation rates is diminished. Of course, good advising, tutorial services, and other services may increase the rates, but the point is that these are interdependent variables that reflect a process and a system. These can be changed and thus the outcomes can be changed. A school could become very selective, admit only the very strongest applicants (those with very high test scores, high school grades, and class rank), and the retention and graduation rates will increase since the issue is systemic.

We can even look at a larger system or process beginning with admissions and look at the impact of this not only on graduation rates, but on job placement rates, career advancement, and alumni giving. All are part of a large, intricate, complicated system, and changes in one area have or normally have an impact on the whole.

We can even look at a larger system or process beginning with admissions and look at the impact of this not only on graduation rates, but on job placement rates, career advancement, and alumni giving. All are part of a large, intricate, complicated system, and changes in one area have or normally have an impact on the whole.

We often state that the Baldrige process forces an institution to look at itself from 30,000 feet and view the organization as a system or series of systems that are interdependent and sensitive to changes. Normally these examples clarify that a process is a way of accomplishing something rather than just citing what has been done and that a system is a process or a concept with many interrelating parts that when put together represents something whole.

Question 8

How do you align all of the systems and departments into a coordinated approach?

Answers

John Conyers; District 15 If organizational improvement is to be truly effective, all facets of the organization must be aligned in the same direction. Problems are usually created by misaligned or, in some cases, nonexistent systems. Misaligned systems occur when people don't understand the organization's goals or directions, so they don't really know what they are expected to do. If they don't know where they're headed, it's hard for them to stay motivated and maintain a good attitude and even harder for them to perform at an optimal level. When employees try to function in a misaligned system—even when they do their very best—all you get are random acts of improvement that can give an organization a false sense of accomplishment.

When employees try to function in a misaligned system—even when they do their very best—all you get are random acts of improvement.

We had always allowed our schools a significant degree of autonomy, but now we were asking them to use their compasses to navigate on the same course as the district. Deming created a flowchart to demonstrate the components of a system that produces something of value. Lee Jenkins offered a wonderful variation on Deming's flowchart to describe education as a system. We began to fill in the specifics of the Jenkins flowchart to describe the major variables that influence the education system from our perspective, including where the School Improvement Plan fit into that system. The theories senior leaders were using in the district were creating less-than-terrific results—perhaps because theories have to be applied in a framework of alignment for there to be any chance of success.

We made sure we had clear and measurable goals and purposes. Our mission statement was also measurable, for if not, it wouldn't have been worth having. We also aligned customers, feedback, the aim of the organization, suppliers, input/output, and processes to manage the organization and continually improve.

We made sure we had clear and measurable goals and purposes. Our mission statement was also measurable, for if not, it wouldn't have been worth having. We lived by the quote by Harry and Schroeder: "Organizations that do not measure what they profess to value don't know much about what they value." We also aligned customers, feedback, the aim of the organization, suppliers, input/output, and processes to manage the organization and continually improve.

There were several steps we followed to get to full district alignment:

1. Ensure that the senior leaders in the organization truly understand the Baldrige Criteria. To apply the Criteria effectively, a high-level understanding of the focus of each category and the linkages between categories is necessary. Senior leaders were expected to speak as one voice about what the Baldrige Criteria are, why the district adopted the Criteria, the key characteristics of the Criteria, and what they will do for the organization. I sealed the agreement with administrators by creating a set of talking points so that we would speak with one voice.

2. We established a clear and compelling mission/vision or purpose for the organization that was developed by listening to the voice of our customers.

3. We then operationally defined goals that, if achieved, would guarantee that the organization would accomplish its mission. An operational definition identifies what needs and expectations the customer has and at what level those needs and expectations need to be met in order to satisfy (or even delight) that customer. These operational definitions became the goals or objectives to be incorporated into what we called "the superintendent's balanced scorecard" to be used by senior leaders to monitor organization performance.

4. We also used the online One-Page Planning and Performance System, available commercially (for more information, go to http://www.onepagebusinessplan.com). Caution: We learned that when deciding to use a scorecard, vision, mission, goals or objectives, and plans for improvement, all of them must be aligned with each other.

We learned that when deciding to use a scorecard, vision, mission, goals or objectives, and plans for improvement, all of them must be aligned with each other.

5. We also aligned job descriptions and work performance to the operational definitions. We worked hard to ensure that every staff member in the organization was on the same page to achieve the operational definitions and accomplish the district mission.

6. The last step of total district alignment was to assure that leaders and staff (including the superintendent) were evaluated on the basis of job descriptions and operational definitions that were now aligned.

7. And finally a strategy that we used successfully for increasing ownership in the principles and practices of continuous improvement was the creation of category champion teams, a process we adopted after benchmarking other Baldrige Award winners. The category champion teams correspond with the seven Baldrige Criteria categories, and they are responsible for how the Baldrige Criteria are applied within an individual category. These teams helped assure alignment with the organization's mission, key goals, board goals, and related student performance targets.

The bottom line is that organizational alignment is the key to improved results. If you are an administrator and a senior leader, check your pockets! You hold the key to your organization's success.

The bottom line is that organizational alignment is the key to improved results.

Richard DeLorenzo; Chugach In the Chugach School system we did not just tweak an obsolete system (i.e., block scheduling, attendance policy, curriculum adoption), we entirely redesigned many of the things that were preventing our students and teachers from being successful. This meant challenging state and federal regulations and initiating new policies that would have the greatest impact. What is incredulous is that research clearly points to what must be done, but overcoming the inertia of traditional schools perhaps poses the greatest obstacle. Winning the Baldrige helped validate that we were on the right course. Table 1 shows some of the changes we initiated that would impact our students' success.

Table 1 Highlights of some of the Chugach School District systemic improvements for students.

Pre-Baldrige	Current System
Institutionally centered	Student centered
Credits or "seat time"	K–12 performance-based system (first K–12 public school system in America to accomplish this)
Lecture-style instruction	Presentation based on student learning styles
Unclear expectations	Precise targets P-14
Disconnected reporting	P-14 report card
Traditional assessments	Skills-based, self, analytical, contextual assessment
Textbook-based curriculum	Contextual curriculum
Poor school-to-life plan	Comprehensive school-to-life plan
Traditional diploma	Performance-based diploma

Joe Alexander; Monfort We found it necessary to develop a visual diagram (see Figure 15) of our organization in order to help us do just that. We call it our Student-Centered Process Framework, even though some of our students have labeled it the "MCB football field."

We found it necessary to develop a visual diagram of our organization in order to help us do just that. We call it our Student-Centered Process Framework.

This visual diagram has become a simple, yet powerful tool for communicating.

This visual diagram has become a simple, yet powerful tool for communicating to our internal and external audiences what our basic production process is and which are the primary components we seek to manage for driving improvement. Through this diagram, we can tie together our management control systems, our strategic planning activities, our various stakeholders and partners, and even our performance indicators.

Furthermore, our diagram is probably not that different from what could be applied to most any educational entity. The various components do not generally change all that much, whether an organization is a school, college, or university.

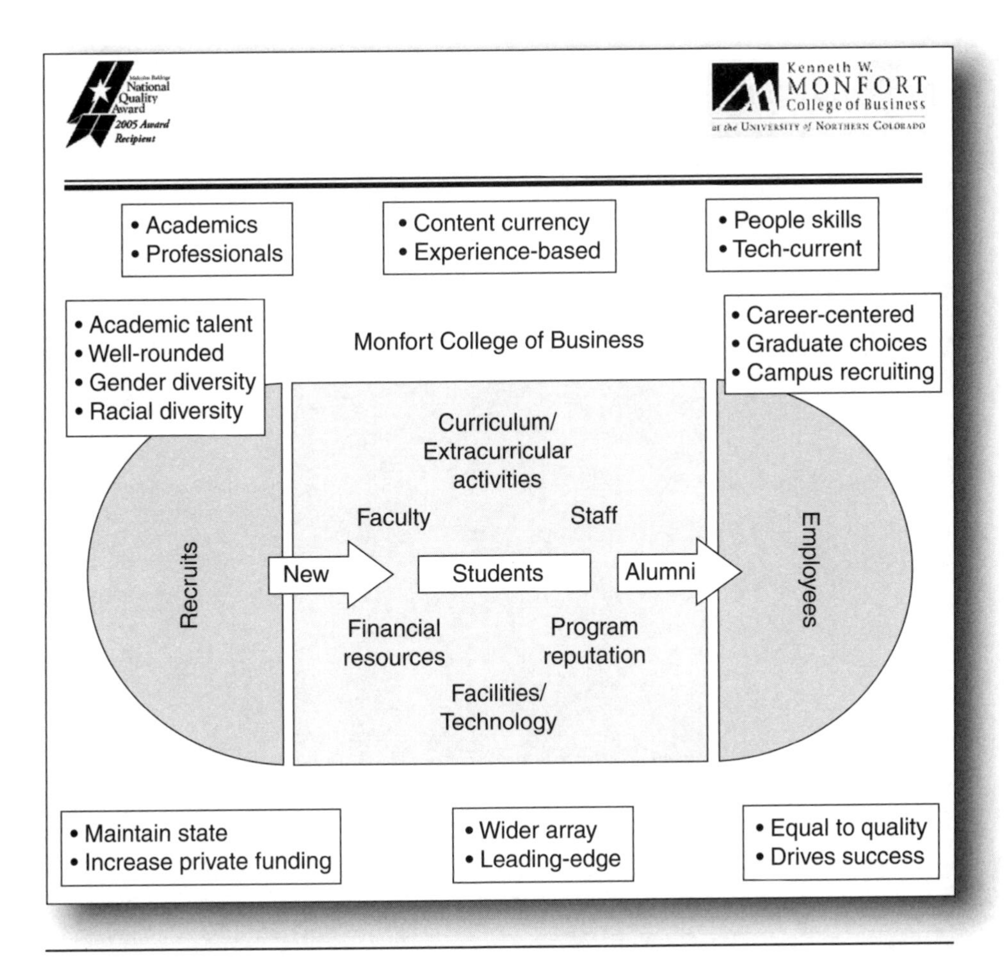

Figure 15 Monfort Student-Centered Process Framework.

Question 9

What were your two most powerful initiatives/actions to achieve success and what were your two biggest mistakes?

Answers

Kirby Lehman; Jenks The two most powerful initiatives or actions were the following. One, several years ago we created the district's Continuous Improvement Leadership Team. This group has served as a focus group for the entire district, helping to strive toward the district's goals and strategic objectives through setting in place a very comprehensive plan of action . . . and sustaining that plan. Two, the actual decision to apply for the Baldrige Award was, in effect, a monumental call to action throughout the district. That decision resulted in a district-wide revitalization of evaluation, planning, and action.

There were mistakes or, at least, changes we would make if we were to do the same thing again. One, there would be direct, early-on discussions with the district's union leadership regarding consideration of implementing the Criteria and applying for the Baldrige Award. Delaying such communications, however briefly,

There would be direct, early-on discussions with the district's union leadership.

Involvement does not always equate to positive support, but involvement does negate criticism such as "but we did not know."

only causes some parties to feel they have been left out of the process. Involvement does not always equate to positive support, but involvement does negate criticism such as "but we did not know." Two, we would introduce some changes more slowly. In the improvement process, it is easy for leaders to become impatient because we often have information that other members of the institution do not possess. Therefore, everyone needs to be brought along at least somewhat at his or her own speed. The second time around we would gather the troops better and bring everyone along as simultaneously as possible.

Richard Maurer; Pearl River The first initiative was the creation of Tristates Curriculum Consortium. Our former superintendent, Dr. Michael Osnoto, was instrumental in starting this. This is a New York, New Jersey, and Connecticut consortium of about 36 high-performing school districts. Membership is by application and is generally restricted to high-performing districts in the tristate area of metro New York City. Its focus is to serve as a critical friend to each other.

The chief function of Tristates is to allow member districts to audit each other's curriculum. Typically, every three years a member district asks the consortium to evaluate a specific curriculum unit K–12. The way this works is that about 25 teachers and administrators, all trained in the evaluation model and process, come to the district and audit the curriculum over a three-day period. The audit centers around 16 specific criteria organized within three central areas. Although the model itself is copyrighted, one can assume that within the area of instructional focus the use of longitudinal data would be one area of evaluation. Each area is rated on a scale of 1 to 5 using a Baldrige-like process of Approach, Deployment, and Results. The criteria are so stringent that few well-accomplished districts ever achieve but a few level 5's. The evaluation team writes a comprehensive feedback report listing the strengths and areas of improvement for each criterion. The district receiving the audit then has to decide which of the recommendations it will focus on. In two years a small group of the original auditors will return to the district to determine how progress has been made. The model is so successful that it has been accepted by the regional accreditation agency, the Middle States Association of Colleges and Schools, as a valid process to achieve accreditation.

I was part of Tristates in the Pearl River School District and served as codirector of the consortium for two years while I was superintendent. The Ardsley School District was not a member of Tristates, but within a year of my arrival it applied and was accepted as a member. At this writing, Ardsley just completed its first audit, and it was in the area of K–12 social studies. What I found with Tristates is that the model is a close parallel to the Baldrige processes. It shares the same rigor of aligning district mission and values to district planning and action steps to achieve successful results. It provides for critical external feedback by trained experts, and it produces a feedback report that provides specific areas of improvement focus. The difference is that Tristates focuses on curriculum, and Baldrige focuses on organization. The Tristates process is congruent with Category 6 of the Baldrige application, "Process Management."

The use of the Tristates process provides an excellent method to train staff, particularly teachers, in how to use a continuous improvement model. Tristates evaluation is a journey that staff partakes as it prepares for the visit by the expert team. Typically, six months' preparation is needed in gathering evidence to support the criteria required of Tristates. The discussions, study, and products produced to show to the evaluators provide staff with a rich discussion, sharing, and analytical evaluation of their own curriculum and instruction. The Tristates evaluation, like receiving the Baldrige Award, is the end of a long process of self-improvement.

The second initiative I found valuable was the creation of category champions. Early on I involved administrators in the process. I asked each to become expert in one category area, such as surveys, strategic planning, support processes, etc. They were asked to recruit a teacher or two to help them. This pyramid scheme, as you call it, allowed the study process to reach deeper into the organization. It was a benefit in that my senior administrators did not have to do all the work. Often the category champions were the ones who came up with the initiative, the application, or the deployment of the particular Baldrige process. My only regret is that I should have embedded category champions earlier in the implementation of Baldrige. Their buy-in and, more importantly, their contributions would have flowed earlier. The implementation process would have been easier.

I should have embedded category champions earlier in the implementation of Baldrige. Their buy-in and, more importantly, their contributions would have flowed earlier.

John Conyers; District 15 Our biggest mistakes: We should have worked harder to ensure that the community at large knew how important the Baldrige Criteria were to the overall quality of the school district so that when other administrators and board members came to the district, they would have the courage and the will to sustain the continuous improvement process. Also, we should have begun examining process management earlier.

We should have worked harder to ensure that the community at large knew how important the Baldrige Criteria were to the overall quality of the school district.

Joe Alexander; Monfort Getting everyone "on the bus" at the beginning of our journey was clearly the most powerful thing we could have done as an organization (and did) to position ourselves for success. This would apply first to the initial decision in 1984 to move to an undergraduate-only market focus, but more recently to our decision in 2002 to begin implementing the Baldrige framework within our college. Even though in the short run it took more time and energy to work toward the goal of consensus on these decisions, having all of our employees committed to the same goal and aligned toward a single purpose was indeed a powerful thing.

I would say that the second most powerful set of actions we pursued was to expand our workforce, in a sense, by significantly enhancing our partnerships with those university stakeholders upon which we were most dependent. The successful performance of various university units such as the admissions office (i.e., student recruiting), the Foundation (i.e., development and fund-raising), and the library (i.e., curriculum and research support for faculty) were critical for our college being successful on a number of key performance indicators. By formalizing our partnerships with these units into a system whereby we held joint monthly meetings with each for the purposes of increasing each other's effectiveness, we found that this practice made all of us more productive.

The second most powerful set of actions we pursued was to expand our workforce, in a sense, by significantly enhancing our partnerships with those university stakeholders upon which we were most dependent.

Last month, three years into this revised partnership system, I was in my office on a Saturday morning doing some catch-up after a week of being out of town. The phone rang, and I noticed on the caller ID that it was our assistant director of admissions on the line. I answered with a bit of surprise that he would be at his office on a Saturday a.m. He had seen my car in the parking lot, and his reason for calling was that our automatic monthly meetings on MS Outlook had expired and we had skipped a month, something I had not yet noticed. He then expressed how much he had come to value what his office got out of our partnership, and he wanted to make sure we got another year's worth of time slots protected on our calendars so that he did not miss out on any more of our sessions. After hanging up the phone, I sat there in my office and the realization hit me that we had in fact crossed a major milestone in that our partners were now just as dependent upon our meetings as we had been at the beginning. That was a very rewarding Saturday!

As for biggest mistakes, the first that comes to mind is in regards to how quickly we attempted to implement things. When we made a commitment to adopt the Criteria and begin work on our formal application was in the fall of 2002. We decided that since there were two months in between the state (i.e., Colorado Performance Excellence) and national application due dates, we would do both in the same annual cycle. We received both sets of initial feedback in early fall of 2003 and repeated the same process in spring of 2004 before receiving the Baldrige later that fall. In retrospect, this translated to four separate formal feedback reports, countless opportunities for improvement, and not near enough time to make the adjustments called for based on the volume of examiner feedback within the limited time window.

Even though the path we took by doing the state and national applications simultaneously was the quickest path toward the awards and being able to observe evidence of progress based on improvements made, I do think we missed out on some of the improvement opportunities we could have acted on, simply because we were receiving feedback faster than we could process it in some instances.

To me, the path that organizations like Branch Smith Printing followed through multiple years of application at the state level, followed by multiple applications at the national level, would be the recommended model for an organization.

The other most instructing mistake I have observed for us now that I see more clearly from hindsight is in regards to the lack of examiner employees which we had within our organization as we went through the initial implementation phase. When we began in fall 2002, we had only one Baldrige examiner as an employee and zero examiner experience at the state level. If I had it to do over again and could have planned ahead more successfully, I would have served as an examiner myself prior to our having begun formal application, and I would have also attempted to have placed as many individuals as possible from my leadership team into examiner training. I think this would have solidified our internal understanding of the Criteria much more readily, and I think that such a practice would have given us quick access to more best practices from the organizations our employees examined.

Steve Mittlestet; Richland College Narrowing our organizational strategic planning priorities for student learning to the most important four (response to community, student success, employee success, institutional effectiveness), with 16 related key performance indicators and their measures, with both leading and trailing components, has allowed our executive team to conduct meaningful, action-oriented monthly balanced scorecard reviews that can deploy resources focused on targeted areas of need without micromanaging and without initiating sweeping initiatives that upset the good work of organizational entities that are achieving according to plan. This strategy allows us also to move quickly and innovatively when unanticipated mission-related opportunities arise or are created because we know where these initiatives can fit in the big picture and the impact they will have on resources.

Narrowing our organizational strategic planning priorities for student learning to the most important four . . . has allowed our executive team to conduct meaningful, action-oriented monthly balanced scorecard reviews that can deploy resources focused on targeted areas of need without micromanaging and without initiating sweeping initiatives that upset the good work of organizational entities that are achieving according to plan. This strategy allows us also to move quickly and innovatively when unanticipated mission-related opportunities arise or are created.

One of our biggest oversights was not insisting that all members of the executive team be trained as examiners early on, as their learning, relative enthusiasm, and ability to deploy the work was much slower than for those of us who received the training on the front end.

Question 10

Can I implement just some of the Baldrige Criteria rather than address all the questions at once? And if yes, which is best to begin with?

Answers

Kirby Lehman; Jenks In order to get some institutional buy-in, if there is a plan to introduce only part of the Criteria, implement those Criteria concepts that are most closely aligned with what your institution is currently doing successfully—especially if there is heavy staff involvement in and ownership of that specific part of the system.

Richard Maurer; Pearl River It is best to begin by introducing the Plan-Do-Study-Act model (PDSA) as a means to implement change in the district. The PDSA model is based on the scientific experimental method meaning first one plans or sets up a hypothesis, then one conducts an experiment to determine if the hypothesis is true. If the hypothesis is not true, then one needs to study the data from the experiment and make necessary adjustments. The PDSA is at the heart of any continu-

The PDSA is at the heart of any continuous improvement process.

Month	Task	Function
June	Gather baseline assessment data	Plan
Summer	Analyze data, develop plan to address gaps in performance	Plan
September–October	Implement plan	Do
November–December	Check on progress with a formative assessment	Study
December–June	Modify implementation plan, roll out new plan	Act

Figure 16 Pearl River planning process document.

ous improvement process. It is easy to explain and easy to illustrate. Most school districts have a planning process that begins in September of the school year and concludes in June of the following year. This planning process can be seen as a type of PDSA. Figure 16 explains how the planning process to incorporate a new elementary phonics program can use a PDSA model to assure success.

PDSA can be used in any strategic endeavor and can be easily illustrated. This allows everyone involved to be aware of the process, at what step the process is functioning, and how to make quick adjustments to the plan so that success can be achieved. It is important to consider what would happen if the PDSA process was not used. In such a case for many districts, a new phonics program would be bought for every teacher in the elementary school(s). It would be required curriculum. There would be some level of training, but because of the huge rollout, the training would be inconsistent at best. Errors with the deployment would surface, as would happen with any innovation, but because of the massive investment of time, energy, and money, it would be impossible to fix or make important modifications. As a result, teachers at the grade level would begin to make their own modifications to make the curriculum fit into what they are already doing. The original intent of the curriculum designer is now lost, and the phonics program is different than that planned. When reading scores do not increase at some later date, folks begin to look for reasons why. They may blame the student, the teachers, or the curriculum unit itself. Since the students and teachers cannot be changed, the folks in charge change what they can—the curriculum. So in subsequent years a new phonics or new reading program is introduced, hoping for success. And so the cycle of failure continues.

Richard DeLorenzo; Chugach I believe we have many fine managers in American schools, but very few innovative leaders who are willing to put their career on the line each day to lead us where we need to go. Thus, a shared vision that includes all stakeholders and that is driven by a sustained framework of excellence is where we *must* aim. This education system of the future must have the capacity to repeatedly reinvent itself as needed—an innovative system that puts children's needs first and benchmarks internally and externally to demonstrate positive trends that will lead us to becoming world class.

John Conyers; District 15 You cannot have a casual relationship with the Baldrige Criteria. The performance questions and Criteria force you to drill down in your organization by collecting and using data. Flirting with the Criteria won't get you the solid results you need. However, if you are dealing with some major resistance factions, it is better to start somewhere than to do nothing at all. Begin with alignment, alignment, alignment—but understand that aligning the organization will violate people's comfort zone. No organization can be aligned if it does not have a mission, goals, and performance targets.

Flirting with the Criteria won't get you the solid results you need.

Begin with alignment, alignment, alignment—but understand that aligning the organization will violate people's comfort zone.

Joe Alexander; Monfort In short, you "can," but why would anyone want to? The real power in the Criteria is when it is viewed and utilized together as a system. Senior Baldrige examiner John Latham is fond of using the analogy of a chess board and its pieces to explain the power of understanding and utilizing the entire Baldrige system for improving one's organization. There is obviously some inherent power in understanding the movements and strategic uses of an individual chess piece (e.g., knight), but to understand the roles and capabilities of all pieces as part of a coordinated strategic framework is exponentially more powerful.

I would think an organization would be better served in the long run to have begun implementing all of the Baldrige Criteria as a system, even if at an introductory level, than to have become an expert in one area before starting on the others.

Charles Sorensen; UW-Stout The power of the Baldrige Criteria is the comprehensive structure they provide for organization management, as well as the fact that they do not mandate an implementation sequence, thus allowing organizational discretion to implement the Criteria sequentially, in parallel fashion, or selectively.

Since most higher education organizations have long-standing traditions and cultural expectations, it is best to begin with a high-level organizational self-assessment using the Baldrige Criteria. At UW-Stout this was facilitated by a senior Baldrige examiner. At this daylong meeting, senior management identified processes and systems that aligned with the Baldrige Criteria and also substantive gaps that needed to be addressed. After a self-assessment, an organization can then choose to nurture the organizational units demonstrating strengths and alignment with the Criteria to develop a grassroots approach, or it can look at organization-wide initiatives.

UW-Stout chose to implement organization-wide initiatives in the areas of leadership and planning. Our choice was influenced by the external pressures bearing on higher education, most of which still exist today, including declining state support, a demand for increased efficiency and effectiveness, the effect of technology on instructional pedagogy, and the decline in respect for higher education in general. We also considered that our institution had strong programs and systems in place to monitor stakeholder needs and was achieving high satisfaction ratings as well as demonstrating resource efficiency. Most importantly, we felt that organizational transformation could occur only with strong leadership and strategic planning systems.

The importance of an effective leadership system cannot be minimized. Whether an institution deliberately structures its leadership system, the values of the leadership team, and the expectations for the group or allows that to occur informally, a leadership system does exist. UW-Stout chose to structure a distributed leadership system which for our organization means a sharing of responsibility and accountability. Over time I made changes in the leadership team to assure the right people are "on the bus" and have an appreciation for the values and direction of the institution. Creating an effective leadership system also encompasses building a team environment. At UW-Stout this is accomplished purposefully—as a team attending professional development sessions in leadership, administration, and management; discussing emerging issues; visiting Baldrige recipients and other innovative organizations; and inviting outside leaders to visit with the group.

The importance of an effective leadership system cannot be minimized.

As an effective leadership system was being implemented, we were also designing a strategic planning system that built upon the commitment of the leadership group, provided adequate planning support, engaged the campus community and external stakeholders in an open, participatory way, and allowed for multidirectional communication. The planning system is characterized by fall listening sessions with the campus community, identification of longer-term and near-term goals, development of action plans to deploy initiatives, agreement on performance indicators to evaluate success, and alignment of budget allocations to university action plans. The performance indicators shown in Figure 17 are used to evaluate success of the action plans.

The university focuses its planning efforts in the following major areas: academic, diversity, information technology, alcohol and drug abuse prevention, marketing, capital budget, and annual university priorities.

As a result of this implementation strategy to strengthen the leadership and planning systems at UW-Stout, we have been able to engage in transformational initiatives. A couple of recent examples include our e-Scholar program, which provides each student a laptop computer and infuses digital technology into most aspects of student living and learning, and most recently our FOCUS 2010 initiatives that include achieving polytechnic designation for the institution through institutional strengthening of characteristics common to polytechnics.

Performance Indicators
1. Enrollments
2. Transfers in
3. Tuition rates
4. Tuition revenue
5. Retention rates
6. Student engagement (National Survey of Student Engagement)
7. e-Scholar learning measure
8. Student satisfaction survey
9. Distance education courses/programs
10. New, revised, and discontinued academic programs, and certificates
11. Faculty research
12. Overall morale
13. Safety
14. Energy efficiency
15. Graduation rates
16. Placement rates
17. Employer ratings of student technology skills

Figure 17 UW-Stout performance indicators.

Most institutions implementing the Baldrige Criteria discover the strong relationship among the categories that eventually results in full implementation. The leadership triad (leadership, strategic planning, and stakeholder focus) interact with the process triad (human resources, process management, results), and this entire system is dependent on a foundation of information and analysis.

Steve Mittlestet; Richland College I would recommend that an organization start with a Baldrige self-assessment to find obvious performance gaps and determine whether these gaps are in high-priority areas where investment of time, energy, and resources will yield an obvious and immediate return. Once determined where to begin, have the leaders of the appropriate groups receive examiner training and participate in application reviews and site visits to grasp more fully how the Baldrige discipline can benefit their organization. Ideally the CEO and other executive leaders would set the examples by being early trainees.

Start with a Baldrige self-assessment to find obvious performance gaps and determine whether these gaps are in high-priority areas where investment of time, energy, and resources will yield an obvious and immediate return.

As soon as possible, have the institution start filing annual applications to the state quality program to begin to receive examiner feedback as an external reading of opportunities for improvement that can be matched against institu-

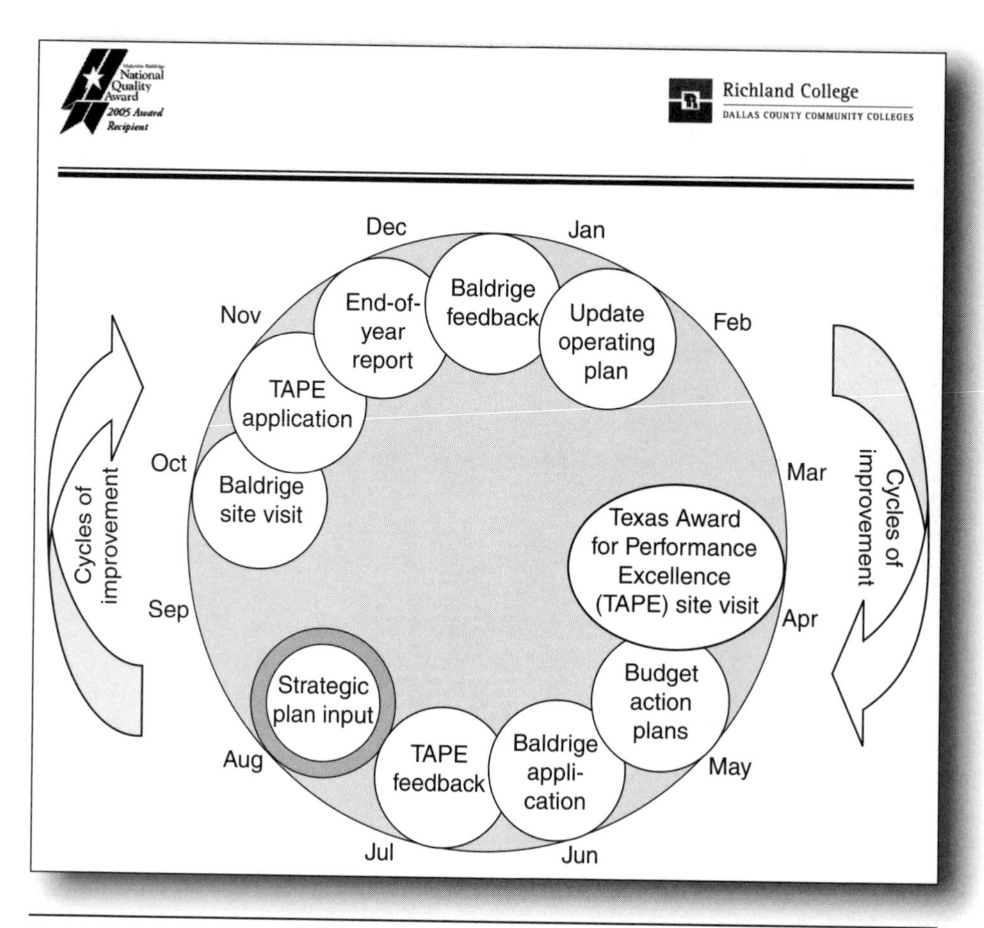

Figure 18 Concurrent annual improvement cycles.

tional priorities. Don't bite off more than your organization can chew, but don't be shy, either. Remember that the Baldrige discipline is about organizational transformation for achieving better mission-related results and overall performance excellence, not about winning a national award. Figure 18 depicts how we manage and integrate multiple external evaluation programs into our annual cycle.

Do not get overwhelmed by the distance between your initial assessment and where you want to be. It is your journey, which can be full of rich intrinsic rewards all along the way.

Achieving your mission-related vision should be your inspiration. Should your organization one day receive the national award, you will then know what all other Baldrige recipients know: the award is a wonderful, public milestone on a long organizational journey toward performance excellence, with many miles yet to go.

Question 11

How do you use Baldrige as an assessment tool? Do you integrate Baldrige with other assessments? How do the Criteria support your required assessments (e.g., student performance, regional accreditation, NCLB measures)?

Answers

Richard Maurer; Pearl River One of the ways I convince the board of education to become involved in the Baldrige process is to talk about it as an audit function. Boards are familiar with what audits do. For example, every board has an external auditor who analyzes the accounting entries to determine if proper procedures were followed and to testify what the true fund balance of a district may be at the year's end. Another kind of audit they are familiar with is curriculum audits. Most school districts have an area of a curriculum evaluated by external or internal means every year. An expert in the field, usually a consultant, comes and after an analysis of the curriculum makes recommendations for improvement. Many districts have curriculum evaluations on a three- or five-year cycle. More recently, school districts are being required to audit their facilities and infrastructure. This is done by engineers or architects, people who are external to the district who have noted expertise.

I try to talk about Baldrige as a process of self-study and analysis of the organization of the district. Typically, board members interpret this as central administration, the

I explain that experts from management and businesses outside of education will be evaluating the district's application according to the seven Baldrige Criteria and that they will provide a feedback report similar to reports boards receive from financial auditors, curriculum evaluators, or facility engineers.

business office, or the principal's office. This kind of audit is appealing to them because it has most likely never been done before. For many board members it is an area they have little experience with unless they are part of management of a large company. The idea that the administration can become better aligned, be more efficient, and more responsive to the educational needs of the district is attractive. I explain that experts from management and businesses outside of education will be evaluating the district's application according to the seven Baldrige Criteria and that they will provide a feedback report similar to reports boards receive from financial auditors, curriculum evaluators, or facility engineers. While the feedback on strengths of a district is nice to hear, the real value in the feedback is in the opportunities for improvement. I explain that the board and the administration look at these areas, discuss them, and decide if they are areas worth working on to improve the organization. My experience is that most, if not all, of the areas are important to improve. But there are also areas mentioned by the experts that just do not fit into the values of the district or are too costly at the present moment, and these can be parked for future look or can be filed in the permanent file. So, whether you call it an audit, assessment, evaluation, or a feedback report, it is all the same. The results, both the self-study to produce the application and the feedback report, help to improve a school district to focus on its core mission and values.

John Conyers; District 15 Baldrige Criteria are extremely sophisticated and thorough when used as an organizational assessment package.

You cannot address NCLB with random acts of improvement. NCLB requires basic system redesign, integration, and alignment to achieve these results. All school improvement plans had to be conducted using the PDSA and root cause analysis format. All other assessments grew out of reviewing the processes that were being assessed in our testing program. Attention was focused on pushing for leading indicators, and not lagging indicators. In other words, focus less on results data and more on quarterly and even daily assessments. We were ahead of the game when NCLB finally arrived because we had been practicing a tougher self-assessment strategy with more leading indicators (real time). We had learned that we had to provide the teachers with data and internal assessment packages that would help them drive instruction based on data they received from students.

We were ahead of the game when NCLB finally arrived because we had been practicing a tougher self-assessment strategy with more leading indicators (real time).

You cannot change the performance of an organization using results data alone. Results data can only tell you what is working and what needs improvement. If your organization cannot express how well a process is performing in the form of a measurement, you do not understand and cannot improve the process (Harry and Schroeder). This information can serve as a benchmark process to judge whether your assessment data are working.

You cannot change the performance of an organization using results data alone.

Joe Alexander; Monfort We wrote four Baldrige applications (two state and two national), which helped us through four separate improvement cycles and to integrate the Baldrige Criteria throughout our management systems. Given that our university is accredited by the North Central Association and our business college is also accredited by AACSB [Association to Advance Collegiate Schools of Business] International, we already had two assessment systems which we were required to integrate to some degree. What we liked about the Baldrige was that it was consistent at the core level with each of our other required assessment frameworks.

Given that our university is accredited by the North Central Association and our business college is also accredited by AACSB International, we already had two assessment systems which we were required to integrate to some degree. What we liked about the Baldrige was that it was consistent at the core level with each of our other required assessment frameworks.

In fact, my observation is that as our other accreditation systems continue to evolve over time, they are converging into what are highly compatible and similar frameworks.

Our philosophy in addressing accreditation standards (or criteria) has been to begin by determining and implementing what is needed to meet a given standard and then moving toward identifying what can be done above and beyond that minimum requirement to improve our program. Satisfying a team of external reviewers is one thing, but the self-satisfaction that occurs from believing that you have maximized performance on a given indicator or system is infinitely more rewarding!

Charles Sorensen; UW-Stout The Baldrige Criteria support UW-Stout's assessment framework. Soon after adopting the Baldrige Criteria, the University of Wisconsin-Stout became a member of AQIP, the Academic Quality Improvement Program. AQIP is an alternative accreditation process offered by the North Central Association's Higher Learning Commission. AQIP was modeled after the Baldrige process, and the program includes similar values, categories, and criteria. Institutions enter AQIP by demonstrating commitment to continuous quality improvement and participate in a number of action projects each year.

The Baldrige Criteria support UW-Stout's assessment framework. Soon after adopting the Baldrige Criteria, the University of Wisconsin-Stout became a member of AQIP, the Academic Quality Improvement Program. AQIP is an alternative accreditation process offered by the North Central Association's Higher Learning Commission.

During the fourth year of an institution's involvement in AQIP, the institution submits a systems portfolio, a document that is very similar to a Baldrige application, with a strong emphasis on student learning. The systems portfolio is evaluated by a team of AQIP reviewers, and feedback is provided to the institution regarding strengths and opportunities for improvement. Through its participation in AQIP, UW-Stout is able to use the Baldrige Criteria as the basis for its ongoing regional accreditation.

Through its participation in AQIP, UW-Stout is able to use the Baldrige Criteria as the basis for its ongoing regional accreditation.

At UW-Stout, the Baldrige/AQIP Criteria provide the basis for assessment at the institutional level. At the institutional level, the university participates in several annual assessments to measure progress toward university goals, including active learning, student engagement, and stakeholder satisfaction. These instruments include the National Survey of Student Engagement, the ACT Student Opinion Survey, the ACT Collegiate Assessment of Academic Proficiency [CAAP] Test, and the ACT Alumni Outcomes Survey. Other key stakeholder groups, including employers and the UW System Board of Regents, are also surveyed on a regular basis. The results of these assessments are shared widely with the campus and posted on the university Web site.

An example of one of these assessments is shown in Figure 19. UW-Stout performs better than peer and national comparisons on the National Survey of Student Engagement in the area of student learning.

The senior leadership team analyzes trends, segments, and comparative data, seeking potential opportunities for improvement. This review occurs each spring as preparation for the university's annual planning and priority identification retreat.

At the program level, academic program directors review data from the institutional assessments and also are responsible for selecting or developing assessment tools to measure student learning and performance. These tools range from standardized examinations to electronic portfolios. The results of these assessments are reported to the provost's office each year and are also reported to

Worked with other students on projects during class								
	UW-Stout					Comparative Data		
	2001	2003	2004	2005	2006	UW System	Masters	National
Freshmen	2.43	2.44	2.44	2.66	2.97	2.41	2.41	2.40
Seniors	2.84	2.74	2.94	2.65	2.98	2.58	2.58	2.51

On a 1–4 scale with 1 = never and 4 = very often

Figure 19 UW-Stout National Survey of Student Engagement chart.

Source: National Survey of Student Engagement

discipline-specific accreditation agencies, such as the Accreditation Board for Engineering and Technology or the National Association for School Psychology, and are included in Baldrige applications and AQIP reports. The general education curriculum is assessed through the ACT CAAP Test and through course-embedded assessments conducted by general education instructors on an annual basis.

The campus has also deployed two systematic review processes that are aligned with the Baldrige Criteria. The Planning and Review Committee reviews all academic programs on a periodic basis. During the review process, the committee obtains input from all key program stakeholders, including faculty, students, program advisory committee members, alumni, and employers. From these data, program strengths and opportunities for improvement are identified. A similar process exists for the systematic review of the support units, such as the library, enrollment services, and the various administrative offices. The committee responsible for this process also surveys users of the support services and also generates recommendations for improvement for each area reviewed.

The campus has also deployed two systematic review processes that are aligned with the Baldrige Criteria.

Question 12

What made the biggest difference in your implementation journey? Was it a person or an event? If an event, was it internal or external?

Answers

Kirby Lehman; Jenks Our school district, through the continuous improvement process, has developed in a variety of ways over the last decade and a half. In fact, based on student achievement, our district is and has been outstanding for a long period of time. However, with reference to implementing the Baldrige Criteria, there was a single person from within the school district who served as a catalyst for the movement, and that person was an assistant superintendent in the area of curriculum. In fact, she has served for several years as the chairperson for the Continuous Improvement Leadership Team, and she is a key person for communicating the Baldrige Criteria and details of the entire continuous improvement process to Leadership Team members and other staff members across the district. Although the district has been outstanding for some time, the implementation of the Criteria began and continued under the leadership of a single assistant superintendent.

Richard Maurer; Pearl River Clearly the most important event in my journey was my special relationship with General Electric Corporation. When appointed a middle school principal in 1983 I had the opportunity to form a school-business partnership with the GE Leadership Development Institute at Crotonville a few miles down the road. This partnership fostered for 10 years while I was principal. As part of the relationship I had the opportunity to take leadership courses with GE managers at the training site. These were GE employees brought from all over the world to the institute to learn the GE values and culture as well as skills to be better managers. In addition to the courses, I had the opportunity to develop professional friendships with many of the managers and trainers on the institute staff. This was during the period GE was shifting its focus from a company that was managed from the top down to one that empowered its employees to make decisions that affected product manufacturing and development. Customers were placed first as a value, and the company began a process of tightly aligning its processes, whether research, marketing, manufacturing, or sales, to deliver a product to satisfy customer needs. During the course work I came to the realization that leadership's responsibility was to ensure that an organization's processes need to be efficiently designed to serve the customer needs and the employee's satisfaction. I learned that the two were not mutually exclusive. In reality, to gain the one an organization needed the other. I was able to apply much of what I learned at GE to my leadership as a principal and later as a superintendent. Later when I was exposed to the Baldrige process I recognized immediately that its continuous improvement philosophy allowed me to incorporate my own leadership ideas and methods I had developed through GE. It was what they called a perfect marriage and gave me the vision of how the processes could be used in public schools.

The most important event in my journey was my special relationship with General Electric Corporation. I was able to apply much of what I learned at GE to my leadership as a principal and later as a superintendent.

In summary I would urge school administrators who are interested in organizational improvement to seek information from the business world. The research from this area is way ahead of that from school administration. The Sunday *New York Times* business section lists the top 10 business books read by business leaders. School administrators should be reading these as well. I require my Administrative Council (AC) members to be reading a common book every year. We discuss parts of it as the first part of our monthly AC meeting. Each year members of my AC visit or participate in workshops sponsored by other noneducational Baldrige winners. For example, I have had workshops on management by representatives from Dell, Xerox, and the Ritz Carlton.

John Conyers; District 15 Without the wonderful support of more than 2200 employees, winning the Malcolm Baldrige Award of Excellence would not have been possible. Employees deserve respect, and almost to a person, they are willing—even eager—to do what they can to improve the organization. Few people bounce out of bed in the morning and say, "I'm going to screw things up at work today." People like to be included in a bigger agenda, and most of all, people respond to a positive work environment where they know their expertise is acknowledged and trusted. The successful culture of high-performing organizations is truly built person by person.

One critical person in our journey was Robert Galvin, at the time president and chief executive officer of Motorola, Inc. When a Motorola brochure that had been disseminated to all the company's employees worldwide came to my attention, its message disturbed me greatly. It implied that America's role as a leader in the global marketplace was at risk unless the American K–12 education system was improved, and quickly! I approached Mr. Galvin directly, and he graciously made the time to talk with me. What he told me was incisive and alarming. For Motorola to succeed in the future, he said, the students who would someday become its employees must be better educated and more prepared for world-class global competition. During our discussion, I was struck by Mr. Galvin's intense fervor for Motorola's Six Sigma quality system. Six Sigma, he explained, was originally created as a continuous quality improvement technique but had evolved into an overall high-performance system driving the company's business strategy. Reflecting on our conversation, I affirmed to myself that we as a school district needed that same quality fervor . . . that same level of commitment to quality for our primary and extended customers. As I have frequently said in public forums, "The passion that drives us as educators, disciplined with criteria for pursuing excellence, is what we owe our children, our communities, our economy, and our future."

Back in the office, I sat down with the district director of planning: "We have to address the issue of systematic quality improvement across the district." We were a good school district, and we worked hard to pursue performance excellence while maintaining the support and trust of our community. We could point to thousands of examples of excellence throughout the district (what we later came to recognize as random acts of excellence), but the overall results were not especially remarkable. What was missing in our board of education goals and our accountability to the community was an unshakable commitment to district-wide quality that would continue to improve over time.

Richard DeLorenzo; Chugach Defining systemic leadership was the most critical component for our organization to accelerate our journey. When people see themselves as part of the solution, remarkable things can happen. Without effective leaders throughout the organization, this journey will only lead to more spinning of wheels. Trying to fully comprehend the concept of leadership that is systemic in nature and can stand the test of time is one of the more daunting tasks facing our public schools. I believe our success was accelerated when we were able to comprehend what it means to help everyone become a better leader. For us there were three steps that led to establishing effective leaders. The first step was to define leadership. We defined it as: *Leadership is inspiring people to move to a different place based on what we value as our vision.* Once we defined

Defining systemic leadership was the most critical component for our organization to accelerate our journey. When people see themselves as part of the solution, remarkable things can happen.

the term, we next had to operationalize it. So the second step was to create a measurable systematic approach in which we could begin to measure what it meant to be an effective leader. The systematic approach includes a Plan-Do-Survey-Act (PDSA) cycle, where we defined leadership at all levels and created a clear road map to help everyone become a better leader. The third step was to recognize that any kind of sustainable initiative needs to be truly systemic in nature. This means the PDSA cycle reaches all participants. Only then when you drill down will there be evidence that all are working on the same work. These three concepts for effective organizational leadership, as simple as they seem, have eluded all but a handful of educational organizations.

Joe Alexander; Monfort I find it difficult to narrow things to a single person or event. In my mind, three significant milestones stand out on our journey to date.

First, even prior to any thoughts of implementing Baldrige, I chose to follow the lead of my two predecessors by inviting our faculty and staff employees to a series of strategic planning sessions at my home. This had become part of our organizational culture over the previous two decades and was a tradition for any new dean of the college beginning his term of leadership.

The first such session for the college was in 1984 at the home of newly appointed dean William Duff and resulted in an organizational commitment to eliminate all graduate programs and focus 100 percent of college resources on a single undergraduate degree program that would become nationally accredited in business and accounting. This marked a strategic long-term commitment to becoming Colorado's best undergraduate business program. Over a six-year time frame, the college invested heavily in its faculty and facilities while narrowing its program focus. The college became the first public university in Colorado to achieve dual AACSB accreditation in business and accounting in 1992—eight years after the original goal had been set.

The next set of sessions in 1994 at the home of new dean Robert Lynch resulted in a set of higher expectations for the college, including expanded fund-raising efforts and the goal of becoming a named college of business through a major capital gift commitment. This goal was realized in 2000 when the Monfort Family Foundation agreed to a $10.5 million financial commitment over a 15-year time frame, with all funds dedicated to providing margin-of-excellence funding to further strengthen the college's undergraduate focus.

When I was appointed dean in 2002, the question was not whether we would meet together as a group of employees to consider what should be done next, but rather *when* we would meet and what were the directions to my house so everyone could be involved in the decisions. All of our employees (not just our faculty but staff as well) were divided into four separate planning groups and scheduled to meet on four consecutive evenings. Each session included a wide-open brainstorming activity to help us envision "what we wanted to be when we grew up" as an organization—or at least what point we wanted to mature to in our evolution as a college. Collectively, we accumulated several pages of information on our flip-chart easel. We then attempted to merge similar ideas and organize the information into a smaller number of categories. As leaders, though, we were still struck by the sheer enormity of how many good ideas were on the table, as well as the ambitiousness of our employees. How could we possibly maintain our commitment to program focus and yet still move forward?

The answer apparently lay in the mind of one of our professors, Sharon Clinebell, who had been a three-time Baldrige examiner. She brought forward the idea that since educational entities were now eligible to apply for the Baldrige Award, maybe that could be a next big goal for the college. Our associate dean at the time, Gerald Shadwick, who as a former bank president had led his organization to a significant national award in that industry, also championed the idea of having such a stretch goal in terms of what it could do to energize and engage our college in moving forward. So it was with this in mind that we began to explore the Baldrige framework as a set of tools for taking our program to the next level. What we quickly determined was that a majority of the employee ideas from our brainstorming sessions aligned directly with an integration of the Baldrige Criteria into our systems and processes. I would say at this point that we were very intrigued as leaders but did not yet "have everyone on the bus," as the saying goes.

The second milestone event on our implementation journey, then, was when we invited Dr. Julie Furst-Bowe from the University of Wisconsin-Stout to visit our campus over a two-day period in fall 2002. During her visit, she met with almost all of our employees in various groups, with the twofold purpose of sharing the UW-Stout Baldrige journey and what all that encompassed, along with developing her own assessment of what our stage of readiness was as a college and whether or not we were in a legitimate position to begin the formal application process. At the conclusion of her visit, she issued a summary statement of "What are you waiting for?"

This assessment, from a senior leader of the only other higher education Baldrige recipient at the time, served as a powerful external testimony to our employees that we could and should take the next steps forward by committing to a Baldrige journey. I also recall that only one of our employees at the time regarded our decision as ill-advised, and his rationale was based on having previously been an executive at a Fortune 500 company that had pursued Baldrige unsuccessfully. So, with approximately 98 percent of our employees "on the bus," we began the process of self-assessment, interpretation of the Baldrige Criteria, and application of quality principles where we identified existing gaps in our systems and processes.

I view the third milestone in our journey as being when we passed the point of concluding our first-annual improvement cycle on our key performance indicators (KPIs) and began to see marked improvements almost across the board.

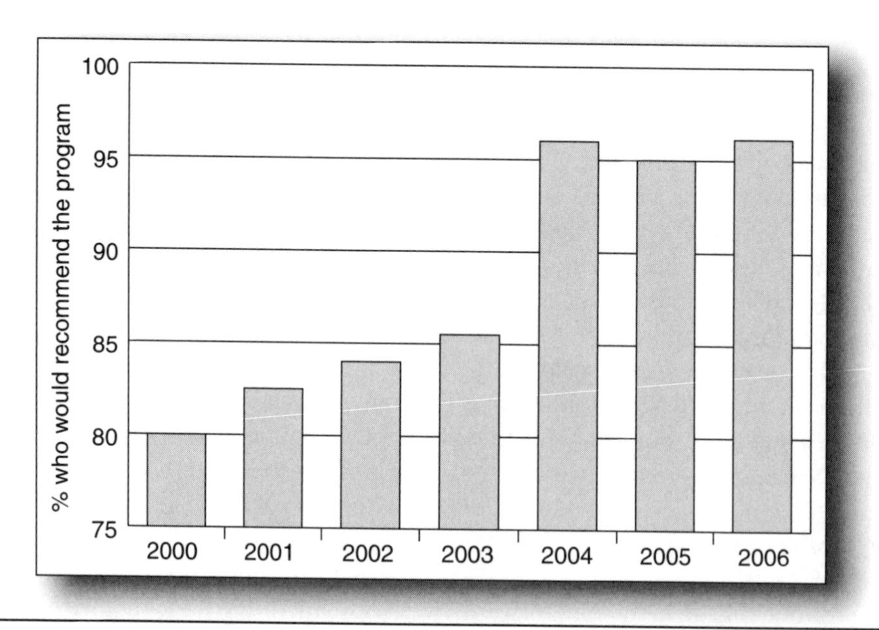

Figure 20 Monfort continuing student satisfaction levels.

In many cases, we noted far more than mere incremental gains—rather, we made significant jumps in our results (see Figure 20).

One notable improvement was in our continuing student satisfaction ratios, where although we had shown consistent improvement, we had never been above 86 percent through 2003. Following the first full year of Baldrige implementation, when we took our annual assessment in January 2004, we had improved to 97.2 percent on this metric. That high score has held since then and even shown additional improvement.

Following the first full year of Baldrige implementation, when we took our annual assessment in January 2004, we had improved to 97.2 percent on this metric.

Another improvement (see Figure 21) was in our student learning results, where we had come close to but never reached the overall top 10 percent nationally on the ETS Major Field Test, which we administer along with approximately 500 other business programs across the U.S. We have now demonstrated top decile results on this assessment for three straight years and cracked the top 5 percent category for the current year.

I think that being able to observe firsthand how our efforts were driving improvement helped to solidify the commitments of anyone on our staff who had previously been even a bit skeptical of the potential benefits.

Charles Sorensen; UW-Stout The University of Wisconsin-Stout experienced a crisis in the mid-1990s which served as a catalyst for change. There were serious concerns on campus involving communication, trust, budget reductions, and decision making, which resulted in a no-confidence vote against top administration during the 1995–1996 academic year. In response to the vote, new systems for leadership, planning, budgeting, and technology management

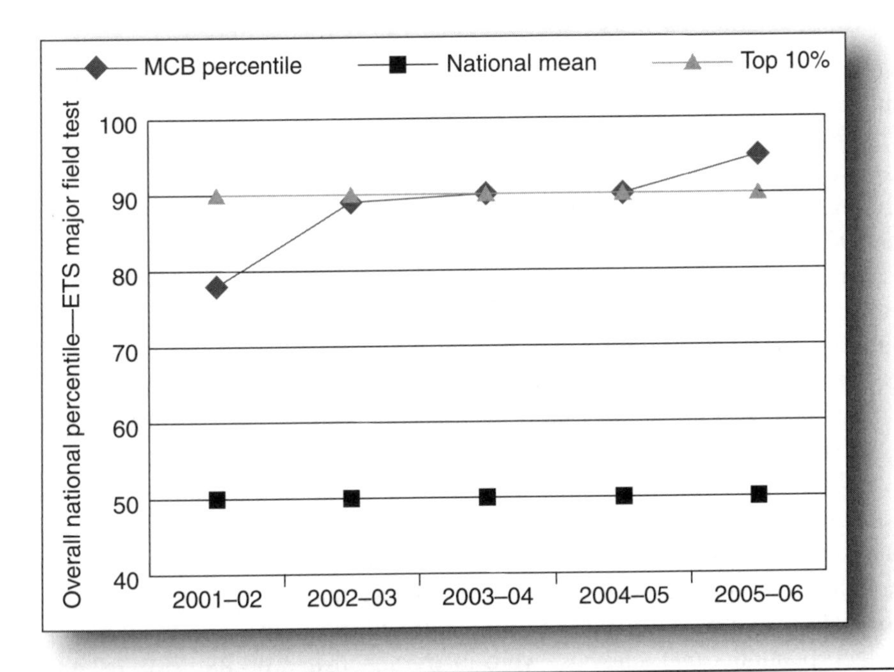

Figure 21 Monfort graduation student learning results.

were implemented in an effort to strengthen the institution and regain the trust of the faculty and staff. By 1998, these new systems had been in place for two to three years, and the early results were promising. The results caught the attention of Roy Bauer, a UW-Stout graduate, a member of the Stout Foundation Board, and, at the time, a senior examiner with the Malcolm Baldrige National Quality Award program. Roy had led the successful Baldrige effort at IBM Rochester, and he was impressed with the progress he was observing at UW-Stout in key process and result areas. He introduced the new Baldrige Criteria for education to the senior leadership team, as he believed the application of the Criteria would allow UW-Stout to move to a higher level of performance excellence.

The University of Wisconsin-Stout experienced a crisis in the mid-1990s which served as a catalyst for change.

Roy Bauer began spending extended periods of time with the senior leadership team, the Chancellor's Advisory Council. He walked the team through the Baldrige values, categories, and Criteria and, in a one-day session, assisted with a high-level initial self-assessment that led to the decision to submit a Baldrige application in 1999. He also assisted with the application writing process, helping the senior leadership team translate the Baldrige Criteria into the terminology commonly used in higher education and assisting in preparing the initial results. That first application moved to the consensus stage of the judging process, and Roy was instrumental in helping the senior leadership team understand and prioritize information in the first feedback report and explaining how to use the feedback to improve systems and processes throughout the university.

When the second Baldrige application, submitted in 2000, went on to the site visit stage, Roy was instrumental in helping the campus prepare for the visiting team. He worked extensively coaching the senior leaders and also spoke with groups of faculty and staff on what to expect from the examiners and the value of this process for the institution. Although the campus was somewhat disappointed not to have received the award following the initial site visit, Roy remained positive and again helped the senior leadership team use the feedback report for continuous improvement. He continued to work with the senior leadership team and other groups on campus as UW-Stout submitted its third Baldrige application in 2001, and the university received a second site visit in the fall of that year. When UW-Stout received the award that fall, he continued to provide advice on the upcoming awards ceremony and Quest for Excellence Conference.

Within the university, there was a small subset of the Chancellor's Advisory Council that worked directly with Roy on the organizational assessment and subsequent development of the three Baldrige applications. These individuals, including the vice chancellor for administrative and student life services, the associate vice chancellor for academic and student affairs, and the director of budget, planning, and analysis, were instrumental in working to translate the "Baldrige-ese" into academic terminology, deploying improvement initiatives, and getting faculty, staff, and administrators on board with the process. Having an external Baldrige-experienced person working closely with members of the senior leadership team who were engaged and committed to the process was the essential element of success.

We held true to our organizational values of integrity, mutual respect, deep caring for one another and our students, and joy.

Steve Mittlestet; Richland College The biggest positive difference in our implementation journey was that we held true to our organizational values of integrity, mutual respect, deep caring for one another and our students, and joy—taking our important life-changing, life-enhancing educational work seriously and ourselves lightly. Figure 22 depicts how these values align and support our mission and vision.

Mission

Teaching, learning, community building

Vision

Richland College will be the:
. . . best place to learn
. . . best place to teach
. . . best place to build sustainable community

ThunderValues

Richland College affirms these values for our learning and working together:

Integrity; Mutual trust; Wholeness; Fairness;
Considerate, meaningful communications; Mindfulness;
Cooperation; Diversity; Responsible risk taking; and Joy

Figure 22 Richland mission, vision, and ThunderValues.

Question 13

What kind of financial impact has implementing Baldrige brought to your organization? In other words, have you been able to link it to the bottom line? Do you have examples of how using the Baldrige approach has saved your organization time and dollars?

Answers

Kirby Lehman; Jenks It would be difficult to identify specific financial ramifications in our district that could be directly related to the Criteria. However, the evaluative procedures we have implemented as a result of studying and working with the Criteria have undoubtedly improved the bottom line in our school district. For example, the evaluation of training that takes place in the district has led to greater focus and economizing in a variety of ways. A greater focus on the safety and health of faculty and staff has had a direct and positive impact on our worker compensation costs. Other evaluative procedures have led to improved economizing in the purchasing procedures used in the district.

A greater focus on the safety and health of faculty and staff has had a direct and positive impact on our worker compensation costs. Other evaluative procedures have led to improved economizing in the purchasing procedures used in the district.

John Conyers; District 15 The costs incurred in implementing the Baldrige Criteria are more than offset by gaining organizational focus (focusing on the right things and *not* what feels good) as well as alignment across the organization. The Criteria force you to ask troubling questions about your processes and outcomes. When you do this, you find that you can actually drop things from your menu of responsibilities. After more than 40 years in education, I found it astonishing that for the first time, we were actually able to drop activities and stop taking on new tasks and financial responsibilities that did not deliver results. An example was when we tackled the issue of aligning curriculum and standards. Our teachers said: "If you expect me to meet a performance target of 90 percent of all students meeting or exceeding state standards, I have to have the time to actually teach these standards." So, we worked with Mid-Continent Regional Laboratory and aligned our standards to world class (16 nations and Third International Math and Science) while looking at the amount of repeat teaching and review. We were able to drop 38 percent of the items in the scope and sequences of most textbooks. (I actually asked for 30 percent.)

By establishing root cause through PDSA, we were able to stop buying programs that did not produce the required results.

By establishing root cause through PDSA, we were able to stop buying programs that did not produce the required results. The money saved was reapplied to the bottom line that stated that in our district, "all second-grade students would *not* leave the second grade *until* they could read effectively."

In every department, we looked at the quality indicators over time using the Baldrige Criteria, root cause, PDSA and Six Sigma, and benchmarking. First, we had to ask our internal customers what they wanted or what results would fit their idea of what quality is, not just occasionally, but consistently.

- We reduced employee attrition by 22 percent, which provided significant savings to the district by reducing the cost of recruiting, training, and monitoring new employees. A recent APQC study indicated that the cost of hiring teachers can run more than $14,000 in some districts.
- More than 13,000 volunteers donated more than 144,000 hours per year to the district. This factored out to be the equivalent of more than 35 professional staff members.
- Survey data showed a 94 percent custodial customer satisfaction rate by teachers in school buildings. Because facility problems were corrected, the buildings cleaned, and technology up and running every day, downtime of teachers and staff was reduced.
- Our benchmarked goal of reducing purchase order time went from 5 days to 2.1 days. The new goal was to be a matter of hours, not days. With a more efficient system, our professionals were able to remain at

their tasks without running around wasting time on unnecessary clerical issues.

- Regular surveys showed a steady increase in satisfaction of working conditions over four years.
- Time and money wasted on labor issues was reduced. We had no grievances that went to arbitration (since 1986), and only two went beyond step one; and we had five-year contracts with all unions.
- Our technology department was able to achieve more than 98 percent network reliability in the classrooms.
- We were able to attain an 85 percent reduction in behavior problems in buses in one year using PDSA and root cause activities.
- The budget development time was reduced by one month.
- Using process management techniques, we were able to reduce the number of board of education meetings from 24–26 a year to 11. This is a tremendous savings of staff time because staffers can now devote time to goal achievement rather than what one of our board members called "the care and feeding of board members."
- Using Six Sigma and cross-functional mapping techniques, we were able to save more than $75,000 on each order of paper in the district—a big savings because school districts run on paper.

Most of all, how can you put a dollar figure on the public relations value of the Malcolm Baldrige Award? Quality instruction and quality programs—and the awareness of that excellence that was generated in our community when the district won the Baldrige—almost certainly had a direct impact on increasing home values in our school district. Realtors told us in our annual meetings with them that not only were families moving into our district for the excellent schools, but also singles with no intention of getting married were buying in the school district because they believed it to be a good investment. We also know that area corporations found relocating employees to the area an easier sell because they could point to our Baldrige Award.

Joe Alexander; Monfort Some will argue that nonprofit organizations, as is the case for most educational entities, do not have a bottom line. Maybe it is due to our role as a business school, but we view all organizations as bottom-line driven—it is just that the overall results may not always be exclusively financial in nature.

Our mission is to deliver excellent undergraduate business programs that prepare students for successful careers and responsible leadership in business. Our performance indicators are therefore tied back to this mission.

For the Monfort College of Business, our mission is to deliver excellent undergraduate business programs that prepare students for successful careers and responsible leadership in business. Our performance indicators are therefore tied back to this mission and include items like numbers of students graduated, overall student performance on national standardized exams, student performance in business competitions against their peers from other business programs, and graduate placement rates within six months of program completion. These indicators are ultimately our bottom line, and I can say that we have observed measurable improvements on each of these items since beginning our Baldrige journey.

As we all know, however, even nonprofit organizations must garner the necessary financial resources to pursue their mission effectively, and this is why we also began working to reorganize our fund-raising approaches in order to better support the quality of programs we could offer.

Included in Table 2 is a list of three supporting performance indicators (SPIs) that our college has tracked for the last several years. The reason I included the two-year comparison that is shown is specifically because it removes the impact of having received the Baldrige Award. The improvements shown were not based on any publicity from having won but rather from the systems changes we implemented to help drive improvement, one of which was an enhanced partnership with our university foundation that plays a key role in our fund-raising success.

As part of our Baldrige implementation, we realized we needed a better working relationship with this key partner and began a regular set of meetings and activities designed to enhance mutual effectiveness. We also realized a need for improved communications with our alumni audience and developed a stronger partnership with the university alumni office. The investments of time and dollars for improving these two key partnerships were more than offset by the results we experienced in our bottom line in that first year alone.

As to whether or not the Baldrige framework has helped us in saving time and dollars, that is a more difficult link to measure. We obviously still have the same amount of time in each day and are equally as busy, it seems, as we were before. But I feel confident in stating that we are spending our time more wisely and have more confidence that as we pursue various initiatives, far more of our efforts are spent on tasks that we can show are tied to mission.

Table 2 Monfort College of Business supporting performance financial indicators, year 1 to year 2 of Baldrige implementation (prior to award).

Performance Indicator	2002–03	2003–04	Percent Change
Total Annual Financial Donations	\$88,738	\$166,189	+87.3
Number of Business Leadership Circle Gifts (≥\$500)	41	43	+4.9
Number of Annual Private Donors (≥\$100)	221	269	+21.7

> *Our bottom line is the balance between stakeholder satisfaction with goods and services and the efficient use of resources.*

Charles Sorensen; UW-Stout Higher education is no different when it comes to improving business operation effectiveness and efficiency. Business as usual really means challenge and change. The Baldrige Criteria help organizations to meet challenge and change by improving organizational performance practices, capabilities, and results. Our bottom line is the balance between stakeholder satisfaction with goods and services and the efficient use of resources.

It does this by encouraging the alignment of organizational performance to student and stakeholder needs, by assessing the continuous improvement of services, reviewing outcomes, and evaluating effective use of fiscal resources.

If we first look at operations management, the Criteria require that we obtain and use student, stakeholder, and market needs and expectations. At UW-Stout, we utilize a wide variety of strategies and processes to assess needs and expectations. These strategies include forums, committees, councils, surveys, reviews, and data collection and analysis.

Community forums are used frequently to solicit feedback and input. We believe in having active participatory involvement. Campus parking is always, well, let me say, a topic of conversation. UW-Stout is a small acreage campus; therefore, parking continues to be pressed to increase its efficiency and maintain rates that will encourage employees, students, and visitors to utilize campus lots rather than congest neighborhood and city streets and metered parking. We recently made a major change to our parking system, a change that has been quite successful due in part to 18 open forums that solicited input from the entire campus community. The end result was the elimination of most reserve parking, which greatly increased the efficiency ratio of each parking space on campus.

We utilize cross-functional committees to provide input, review policies, evaluate programs and services, and identify needs. The Student Center, Recreation/Athletic Complex, and Dining Services all have active advisory committees.

UW-Stout makes extensive use of surveys and other feedback in its continuous improvement processes. Student satisfaction with support services is measured and compared to other universities annually through the ACT Student Opinion Survey. We conduct telephone surveys and even determine the kind of cereal we serve in our food services and the background music we play in the Student Center based on survey results. You may be interested to know that the current cereal of choice for students at Stout is Lucky Charms, followed by Cinnamon Toast Crunch and Honey Nut Cheerios.

Specific support services such as the Student Center, Housing & Residence Life, Information Technology, Physical Plant, and Dining Services participate in national benchmarking surveys conducted through their professional organizations. Survey results are used to improve, change, add, reduce, and/or discontinue aspects of our support services. It also allows our organization to compare our bottom line to other high-performing organizations.

External and internal reviews are an integral part of our continuous improvement process. External food service consultants have been utilized to improve University Dining Service. As a result of the consultant's recommendations, organizational changes have been implemented, marketing efforts have been increased, menus have been changed to better meet student needs and desires, service has been modified, and new products and services have been added.

As a result, satisfaction with UW-Stout's dining services, as depicted in Figure 23, now meets or exceeds the industry average.

Internal reviews of support services are conducted by the Educational Support Unit Review Committee. This committee performs a review of all noninstructional units on a seven-year cycle. The committee provides the university with a way of evaluating whether units are meeting institutional needs and priorities as well as assessing quality and standards of performance and encouraging further planning to improve efficiency and effectiveness.

UW-Stout is a data-driven campus, and data collection and analysis is an important tool for the continuous improvement efforts in our support processes. Data are collected and analyzed for our budget development process, in determining hours of service, for identifying service usage patterns, and in our capital planning process. Data are one of our important building blocks in developing a firm foundation to facilitate continuous improvement. We utilize trend data, data from surveys, financial data, benchmarking data, facility condition data, ratio analysis data, and both internal and external data.

University Dining Performance					
	UW-Stout Trend Data				**Industry Average**
Overall Satisfaction Ratings	**2002–03**	**2003–04**	**2004–05**	**2005–06**	**2005–06**
General Satisfaction	3.8	3.8	3.8	3.7	3.7
Food	4.0	3.9	3.8	3.7	3.7
Menu Variety	3.7	3.5	3.7	3.5	3.5
Service	4.1	4.1	4.0	4.0	4.0
Cleanliness	4.2	4.1	4.1	4.1	4.0
Environment Appearance	4.2	4.1	4.1	4.1	4.1

Figure 23 UW-Stout dining satisfaction, on a scale of 1–5.

Source: National Association of College and University Food Services Customer Satisfaction Benchmarking

College Services	2000	2001	2002	2003	2004	2005
UW-Stout	3.69	3.86	3.70	3.80	3.65	3.74
Public Colleges >5000	3.67	3.68	3.68	3.69	3.69	3.69
National Sample	3.66	3.69	3.69	3.71	3.69	3.69

Figure 24 UW-Stout student satisfaction with college services.
Source: ACT Student Opinion Survey Overall Results 2000–2005

How well does our continuous improvement process work? The Baldrige Criteria indicate that our data should show sustained improvement in satisfaction, loyalty, persistence, and positive referral indicators.

Figure 24 shows UW-Stout student satisfaction with college services. Ratings have been above the public college comparison group each year for the past several years.

Fiscal management is specifically addressed by the Baldrige Criteria, indicating that we need to demonstrate management and effective use of financial resources and recognize the market challenges and opportunities.

Our campus philosophy has always been conservative fiscal management—minimal but steady rate increases—for user charges, segregated fees, and other charges assessed to students. This provides predictability to students, provides a foundation for financial planning, establishes the expectation of fiscal effectiveness, and assures that extraordinary rate increases are planned and have thorough review.

There are many fiscal indicators we use to manage and monitor our business operations. We use our established set of peer campuses, which includes institutions with similar missions, campuses with similar programs, and the other University of Wisconsin campuses.

For example, we review our debt service levels per student and then project using our planned capital needs. Our facility maintenance program provides us the overall condition of buildings. We participate in a number of professional organization benchmarking studies, which provide the comparison to the world outside Wisconsin and guide our actions in keeping abreast of national trends.

Examples of benchmarking studies in which we participate are shown in Figure 25.

We review our cash reserve management position and plan for the long term through our six-year budget plan process.

Our planning process for auxiliaries is comprehensive. Auxiliaries are required to prepare six-year budget plans annually. These plans include a look at past performance, review performance for the current year, provide revenue and rate projections for the upcoming five years, detail by budget category, cash reserve management information, a listing of capital plans, as well as projection of major projects that will need to be bonded. The narrative provided by each

Year	Study	Used to Evaluate/Improve	Partner
1997	Budgeting effectiveness	Financial support processes	APQC
1999–06	Accountability reports	Accountability to citizens	UW System
1995–06	Retention rates	Retention	Integrated Postsecondary Education Data System (IPEDS), Measuring Up, StudentTracker
2000–06	Institutional dining practice	Assess current/future approach	Silver Plate Assoc., National Association of College and University Food Service (NACUFS)
2000–06	Student satisfaction	Organization key processes	ACT
2000–06	Student Learning Practice	Active learning	NSSE/Faculty Survey of Student Engagement (FSSE)/Beginning College Survey of Student Engagement (BCSSE)
2001–06	Leadership/quality practices	Leadership systems	Business Improvement (BI) Company/Fastenal
2003, 2004	University leadership	Leadership systems	National universities
2001–06	Student center/ residence hall	Facilities and services	Educational Benchmarking Inc. (EBI)
2001	Student residence/dining	Student dining/living facilities	David Porter Assoc.
2001	Safety practices	Workplace environment	Hunt Wesson
2001	Diversity best practices	Environment, hiring, retention	Denny's/ProGroup
2004–06	Alumni/graduating senior satisfaction	Teacher education program	EBI
1998–06	Teaching workload	Faculty workload, retention	UW System
2003–05	Information technology effectiveness	e-Scholar program, information technology infrastructure and support	EDUCAUSE

Figure 25 Benchmarking studies.

major auxiliary gives information on current influences as well as a scan of future issues that may impact or alter plans.

Auxiliaries and other business operations must balance the budget and capital needs of the various operations with the student development, programmatic, and personal needs of our students in what is becoming a very competitive market.

The Baldrige model provides a great basis—knowledge of expectations, alignment, effective use of resources, and outcomes—to accomplish this balance between effectiveness and efficiency.

Steve Mittlestet; Richland College With a drop in state funding from nearly 70 percent of institutional costs to 30 percent in three legislative sessions, Richland College had to lower its costs per student contact hour and increase revenue through additional sources. Following the Baldrige discipline, Richland accomplished both increased enrollment and improved results in every key performance indicator including student retention and student learning outcomes. This is shown in Figures 26a and 26b.

Following the Baldrige discipline, Richland accomplished both increased enrollment and improved results in every key performnce indicator.

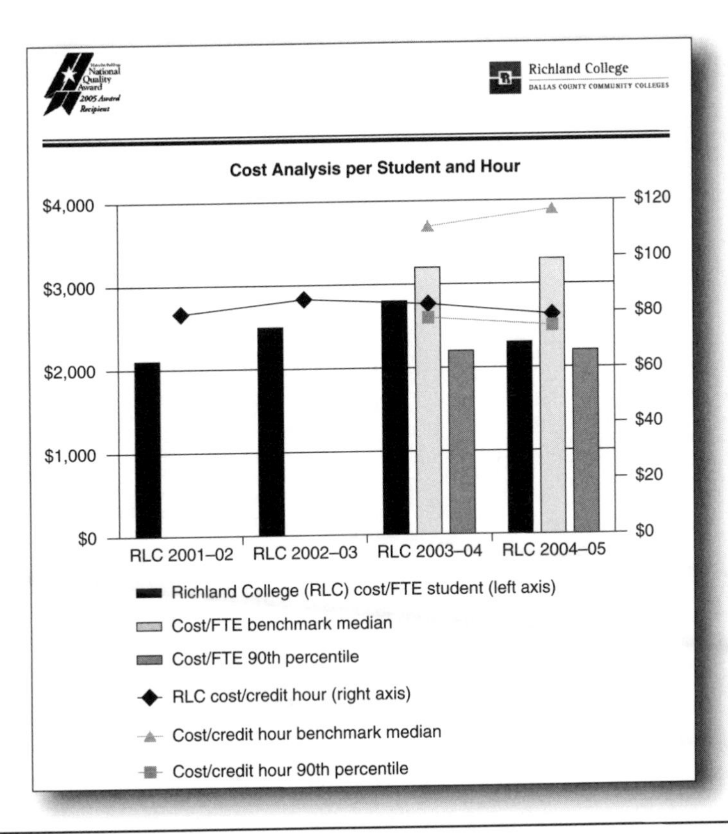

Figure 26a Richland cost efficiency and budget performance.

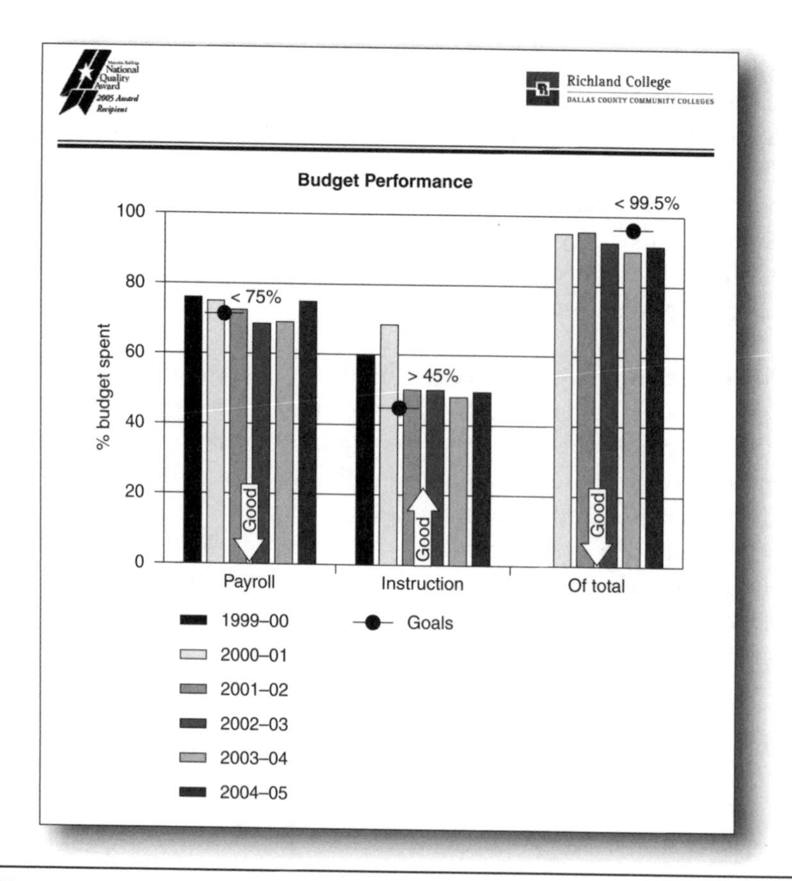

Figure 26b Richland budget performance.

Question 14

What was the biggest headache in implementing Baldrige in your organization and what did you do to overcome it?

Answers

Kirby Lehman; Jenks In our improvement process in the Jenks Public Schools, we began the quality movement by utilizing many of W. Edwards Deming's ideas while referring to that initiative as total quality education, or TQE. Unfortunately, in our school district, sometimes acronyms are not well received. Therefore, when it became apparent TQE would be unacceptable to some of our reluctant staff members, we changed the TQE terminology to "continuous improvement." However, we never changed the direction of our focus or our efforts. We developed a unique Framework for Quality, incorporating three foundational elements (quality training, teamwork, and data-based decisions) under four pillars: quality leadership, continuous improvement, customer focus, and systems/process focus (see Figure 6). All staff members in the district have been oriented to the Framework for Quality and the continuous improvement philosophy of the district. Candidly, it was very difficult for even the recalcitrant staff members to *not* embrace the concept of continuous improvement. Along the way, we took advantage of many opportunities to provide appropriate staff development activities to improve skills in the four pillars and the three foundational areas.

Richard Maurer; Pearl River I would prefer to use the word "challenge" rather than "headache." Getting the different members of the administrative council (AC) to buy into the process was probably the most challenging. For each building principal, assistant, and/or director, there had to be a perceived added value for involving themselves in the process. While the leader has to commit the organization to the process and model it for the AC members, he or she must also find the key to each member so it adds value to his or her work. Let's face it; everyone is busy with tons of demands on time and energy. To announce to the AC that Baldrige is now going to be implemented on top of what they are already doing is going to cause some, if not most, AC members to look very skeptical about the process. The key, then, or challenge, is to help the AC members find value in Baldrige so that the work they are already doing becomes easier or certainly less complicated. Probably a good example is an approach I used with the building principals. Each of them is responsible for collecting and reporting student academic results. Based on this information, most principals are under pressure to maintain or improve high student performance results. In some states, like New York, there is a multitude of state assessments given in most subjects at various grade levels. Now with the NCLB, there are added assessments mandated. For a building principal the responsibility for improving every student's performance on every assessment can be enormous. In fact, no principal can maintain such dedicated energy in this regard. Baldrige presents the building principal with a process that adds value to the task. The strategic planning process, for example, allows the principal to focus his or her resources and energies on improvement for a select few objectives. Rather than saying improvement will occur in all academic areas (and therefore probably none), the Baldrige strategic planning process allows the focus to be a narrow but important spectrum of student achievement. The odds of improvement in these areas rise significantly. The value added for the principal is that he or she knows what the objective is, what resources are being committed, what the plan is, what the implementation strategies are, and what formative evaluative checks will be in place. The work of the principal is focused.

For a building principal the responsibility for improving every student's performance on every assessment can be enormous. In fact, no principal can maintain such dedicated energy in this regard. Baldrige presents the building principal with a process that adds value to the task.

Richard DeLorenzo; Chugach Reflecting on our past, I think one of the greatest challenges in changing an entire school system is the fact that the task seems insurmountable. You just can't seem to get your arms around all of the components that make change systemic and sustainable. The diverse array of

I think one of the greatest challenges in changing an entire school system is the fact that the task seems insurmountable.

variables in any system often leads to a feeling of despair and sense of being overwhelmed and often leads to simply "applying a new coat of paint" and failing to get to the core of change.

John Conyers; District 15 The biggest headache was a perception that kept surfacing—that the district was "good enough." Several times our students' excellent test scores were cited prominently in the Chicago newspapers as among the highest in the state. Our exemplary hiring practices enabled us to draw quality people to the district. As superintendent, I kept hearing people say: "What are you talking about? If it ain't broke, don't fix it." The brutal facts were different, and I knew it.

The biggest headache was a perception that kept surfacing—that the district was "good enough."

Our district's demographics were changing very rapidly. Our district served seven different municipalities where housing ranged from multimillion dollar homes to government-subsidized apartments. We were facing a rising minority enrollment (nearly one-third of our students), a student population speaking almost 80 languages other than English—more than 25 percent from non-English-speaking families. A growing number of our students were from low socioeconomic backgrounds. Complicating the issue was a highly unionized employee culture, with all but a handful of our 2200 employees represented by a bargaining unit. Costs, especially for employee benefits such as medical insurance coverage as well as for goods and services needed by the district, were increasing sharply. Something had to be done, and it was obvious that it wasn't going to be an easy fix.

Joe Alexander; Monfort After we became intrigued as a leadership team that the Baldrige system could indeed make a significant positive impact on our organization if implemented effectively, I would say that our biggest challenge was then convincing our remaining employees and stakeholders that said efforts would be worth the investment of time and energy required beyond their existing job duties.

Our personnel resources were already stretched pretty thin, and the thought of choosing to voluntarily take on new responsibilities and more work was not exactly an attractive option to many within the organization. From a cost/benefit standpoint, what was needed was to somehow paint a clear picture of how the Baldrige system could benefit our college by making us a better organization and translate our actions into better results. I also think that the process of our having to conceptualize how to best articulate that vision to our employees and stakeholders also helped to reinforce in our own minds that we were making the right decision. There's an old saying that if you truly want to learn something, place yourself in a situation where you are required to teach it to others. In the end, the teacher ends up learning more than anyone.

In light of our resource situation, our associate and assistant deans, along with our academic department chairs, agreed that we could not expect to successfully integrate the Baldrige Criteria and write our application by spreading that burden across all of our employees. Most of them were already teaching a full classroom load, pursuing their scholarly research agendas, and fulfilling their regular service portfolio requirements. We had to assure them that while they would be involved in the process, we would not be placing significant additional responsibilities on their backs in terms of time commitments. Our leaders would set the example by committing their time and energy to gathering information and writing the application. If we asked for significant contributions of additional time from any given employee, we would compensate that request by redistributing some of the employee's other duties (e.g., release from a course for one semester or counting a Baldrige assignment toward fulfillment of a portion of the service load).

The ultimate key was to reassure our employees that the long-term goal of our Baldrige journey was to make us a better and higher-performing organization and that the end result would thereby make faculty jobs more rewarding.

In the end, I think the ultimate key was to reassure our employees that the long-term goal of our Baldrige journey was to make us a better and higher-performing organization and that the end result would thereby make faculty jobs more rewarding through the recruitment of better students, better colleagues, better resources with which to do their jobs, and a better reputation for the college. Each of those end products tied to a specific strategic objective held by our college.

Charles Sorensen; UW-Stout When I announced our plans to go forward with a Baldrige application, a decision made by the leadership team, there were faculty concerns that we knew we had to answer satisfactorily before we proceeded. Since the award was developed in the mid-1980s as an incentive for American manufacturers to become more competitive internationally, governance leaders questioned whether an award for the private sector was appropriate for higher education even though NIST had spent years developing the education category. Others pointed out that previous corporate winners had suffered fiscal setbacks after receiving the award, inferring that it may indicate very little about the health of an organization. We listened to the concerns seriously and responded to each one openly and honestly. We first brought in an alum who had played an instrumental role in the success of IBM Rochester's award in 1990. He answered questions and allayed some concerns about the validity of the process. A second and more important decision was critical to gaining campus support and moving forward. We made it clear that we would not open an office of quality or hire new staff to write the application and manage the process. We also made it abundantly clear that we would not in any way change the campus to meet the Baldrige Criteria; either we received the award based on our central mission and how we managed the organization or we would not, but we would not compromise the university for the sake of the award. Finally, we stated very clearly that we would not force the Criteria into the classroom and require faculty to change teaching styles or modify the classroom in any manner. Instead of drilling the process down through academic affairs to departments and the teaching staff, we adopted a macro approach, creating a Baldrige umbrella for the campus and then letting the process be adopted when and where it was appropriate.

In this manner, we won over the faculty and the campus, wrote two applications—1999 and 2000—and then received the award on our third effort in 2001. By not forcing the issue, we had a receptive campus for the site team in 2001 and, after receiving the award, virtually everyone on campus took great pride in this achievement.

Steve Mittlestet; Richland College The biggest headache was self-induced. As state funding for Texas community colleges continued to plummet from nearly 70 percent of instructional costs to 30 percent in only three legislative sessions, I was aware that our publicly funded institution needed to do a better job of assuring our stakeholders more convincingly that community colleges use our resources productively and exceptionally effectively towards achieving our vision of being the best we can be for learning, teaching, and building sustainable community for all. Steeped throughout my life in the humanities, however, I have an abiding skepticism, if not abject antipathy toward being data driven, either personally or organizationally.

In my career I have seen too many examples of people and programs being literally driven over the precipice by knee-jerk actions in response to simplistic analyses of data. I have seen the heart and soul squeezed out of people and organizations in the name of objectivity. The antidote for our data-driven headache, then, was the insight that we could become data informed by "turning to wonder prior to judgment or action" (which has become one of our stated, taught, and regularly practiced organizational values and KPI review principles). This organizational value causes us to ask respectful questions on the implications for data that keep whole people intact and ready, even eager, for responsible risk taking and change.

The antidote for our data-driven headache, then, was the insight that we could become data informed.

Question 15

Winning the award should not be the driver of implementation and commitment to Baldrige—explain how you focus attention on the right things and not the award.

Answers

Kirby Lehman; Jenks One of the primary purposes of the Baldrige Award concept is to bring about quality in our nation's institutions. This would undoubtedly permit America to continue as a world leader in many areas. Thus, the goal behind Baldrige is noble and appropriate. However, quality is not a concept or entity that, once reached, has been achieved—with nothing further to do. Rather, quality is a process which, once in place, must be continued and nurtured toward further improvement. In our district, shortly after being notified of our receipt of the Baldrige Award, our Continuous Improvement Leadership Team met to continue our discussions of future training, to receive a review from leaders who had attended the recent national quality conference, and to further our discussions and studies of an area in which we recognize additional growth is needed: data analysis and usage. In

Such an award reflects just a single step, albeit an important step, in the continuous and never-ending journey toward total quality.

fact, for us, indeed for any institution, the receipt of the Baldrige Award or any other award should not be seen as the "be all" or the "end all." Rather, such an award reflects just a single step, albeit an important step, in the *continuous* and never-ending journey toward total quality. In Jenks, our Continuous Improvement Leadership Team and the entire school district will continue the focus . . . on continuous improvement.

John Conyers; District 15 We learned early on, after winning the Lincoln Foundation Award for Business Excellence, that some people thought, "Now we are done." With continuous improvement you are never done; you can always get just a little bit better. For that reason, we stopped using the word "award" in our oral and written communication and focused instead on the phrase "criteria for excellence." To use Baldrige properly, we found, you have to study it intensely and discuss it constantly in your organization. The Baldrige Criteria are a means to an end and not the end itself. People do not naturally get excited or energized by the Baldrige Criteria. It is a learned process.

The Baldrige Criteria are a means to an end and not the end itself.

Charles Sorensen; UW-Stout I think it is very difficult to separate the process of applying for the award and the incentive to win the award. Our society and culture reinforce at virtually every point that winning is the ultimate goal of any competition. The leadership team focused sharply on the process of continuous improvement as we participated in each of the three application phases. In the first two, we used the feedback report to review our opportunities for improvement, identify peer institutions on a national level, implement some performance measures that we did not then use, and continued to study the data trends. It became very clear to us that the Baldrige worked. We were benchmarking against very excellent schools and performing well in areas such as risk management, energy efficiency, workers' compensation, and so forth.

I think it is very difficult to separate the process of applying for the award and the incentive to win the award. Our society and culture reinforce at virtually every point that winning is the ultimate goal of any competition.

For example, UW-Stout has led the University of Wisconsin comprehensives in efficient energy usage for the past 5+ years, as shown in Figure 27.

We measured ourselves against private sector corporations and companies, even former Baldrige winners, and did well. And, we continued refining and improving our processes. Yet, in the back of our minds remained the simple question, when are we good enough to receive the award?

The journey was worthwhile because we knew we were a stronger organization, were clearly aligned internally, had a great planning process in place, and had a clear sense of who we were and where we were going.

When the call finally came late in November of 2001 from the Department of Commerce secretary Donald Evans

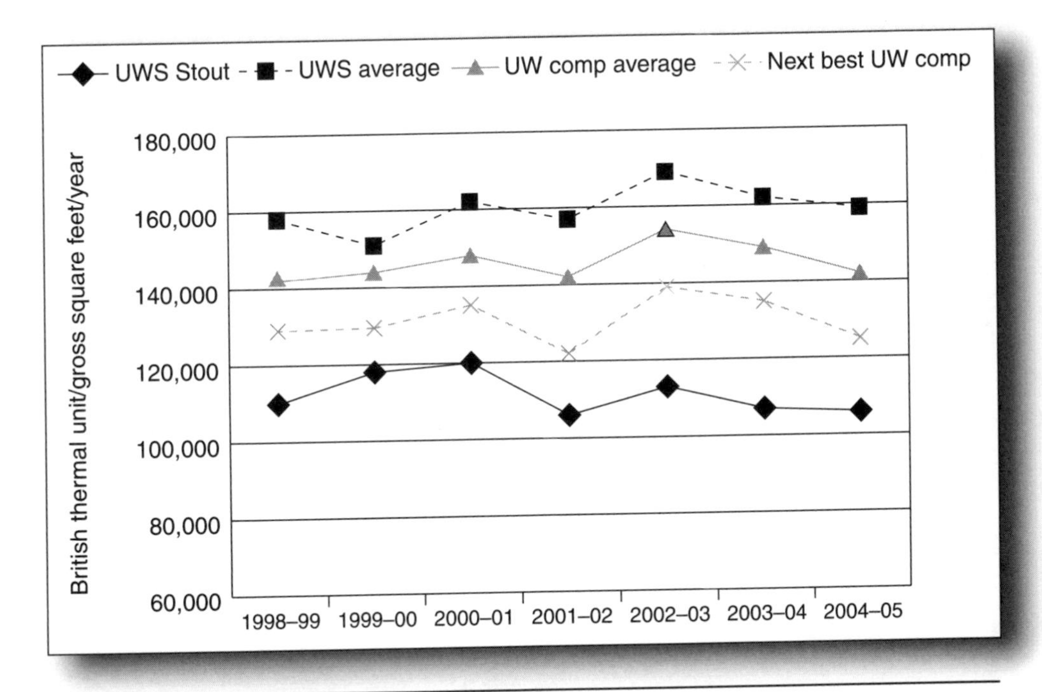

Figure 27 UW-Stout energy usage.

Source: Wisconsin Department of Administration, Division of Facilities.

that we had received the award, the entire team was ecstatic. We all agreed that, indeed, the journey was worthwhile because we knew we were a stronger organization, were clearly aligned internally, had a great planning process in place, and had a clear sense of who we were and where we were going.

I told countless audiences in the months that followed that the journey benefits an organization, but winning is great!

Question 16

Since the time you were selected as an award recipient, how are you continuing your Baldrige journey? For example, tell us about your continuous improvement efforts. How are you using the Criteria these days?

Answers

Richard Maurer; Pearl River One of the unintended consequences of receiving the award was the changeover in school administrators. Some of them retired as part of their career plans, but others were offered promotions in other districts and left. This required a continuous process of training new administrators in the Baldrige Criteria and in the process management steps of the district. Certainly attending Quest was a good introduction, but some of the regional conferences on quality were helpful in transferring the knowledge base to the new administrators. The other issue was the changeover in teaching staff as well. Through retirements, maternity leaves, and adding extra staff because of enrollment growth, administrators had to train new folks in the Baldrige processes as well. Fortunately in New York State, there is a teacher mentor program. This allowed us to match an experienced teacher who knew Baldrige to the new teacher. Still, for a new teacher who has to learn all the skills of effective instruction and learn the curriculum, the additional task of learning Baldrige can be seen as a burden. Also the ability to use the processes seamlessly as part of your professional expertise takes time. This learning curve can take a few years.

Organizations are not static. They change as the nature of any dynamic system that involves as its primary goal service to children, staff, and stakeholders. The Baldrige processes that existed at the time of winning the award need to change as well.

John Conyers; District 15 Sustaining the work of continuous improvement culture is certainly difficult, at best, but not impossible. Having served in four different school districts during my career, I well understand the difficulties associated with change. As I was planning to retire, I established with the board of education a number of specific activities that I would perform to assist the new superintendent in transitioning to the school district and to ensure good succession for the organization. Here are some of those activities.

Normally the current superintendent is not part of the hiring process for a new superintendent, nor did I feel I should participate. However, the board of education asked me to assist with finding a good search company and then, in a casual setting, to participate in interviewing the top three candidates. I was delighted to learn one candidate had previously participated in Malcolm Baldrige training. Although he had not been involved in actually doing a study or site visit, his experience with the Baldrige Criteria was greatly welcomed. When asked by the (then) board of education president for my assessment of the candidates, my comment about him was, "What are you waiting for?" Subsequently, I outlined the necessary succession activities with the district's three assistant superintendents.

We could have sat on the current labor contract for another year, but that would not have been fair to let a new person come in and have immediately to dive into contract negotiations with three separate unions. I worked with the assistant superintendent for personnel and with the board to negotiate new five-year agreements with these unions before leaving the district. That would enable the new person to work on building trust in the organization, have time to get to know people, and let them learn his leadership style.

Over a monthlong period, I introduced the new superintendent to every major community group within the seven municipalities (chambers of commerce, PTA executive board, Rotary Club, etc.). Then I introduced him to every internal group within the district, including union groups and informal groups. It was very important for staff to know that the current superintendent was feeling good about the new superintendent and to let them know that they are in good hands.

Then he and I spent considerable time driving around the total district so he could become acquainted physically with the location of buildings. My travelogue was focused on the history that had transpired over the last 19 years. In particular, it was important to let him know all of the current agreements between library and park districts as well as city agreements that were by handshake only, since it is important that the district keep its word on policy agreements.

Going through each administrator's evaluation was also critical to help a new person know the administrative staff. When some key personnel decisions had to be made before the new superintendent came on board, a meeting was held with the new superintendent and the district executive director to let him know what was taking place. Budget materials and updates, along with reams of other data, were sent to him weeks before he assumed command of the district.

We shared working lunches several times to go over key confidential issues facing the district as well as information on each board member's contribution to the district.

I introduced the new superintendent and his delightful wife to a trusted key real estate person in the district who would help them locate a new home and fill them in on the culture of the community. A call was made to one of our key bankers to pass along a gentle suggestion that a good interest rate would certainly help the new superintendent acquire a new home. This banker had been doing wonderful things for the district for many years, such as supporting our educational foundation.

The district mentor was made available as well, since he had been mentoring all new administrators for several years.

We were basically following a six-phase succession process for senior central office leaders identified in Category 5.1c(3) of our Baldrige application. [See full application on CD.] During the site visit, 30 minutes of interviews with me were about our succession planning. Here are the phases:

1. Confirm the vision for the future of D15 and the major challenges it will face in the next four to five years.
2. Put into place a selection process designed from superintendent and board input.
3. Come to a consensus between the superintendent and board on the criteria for selection.
4. Conduct the search, on a national scale, to find the best candidate for the position.
5. Conduct a broadly scaled interview process to identify the candidate that would best exemplify the core values of D15.
6. Overlap start and stop dates so that newly appointed leaders can spend on-the-job time with current position holders in a coaching arrangement ensuring a seamless transition. I moved out of my office and moved into a small side room next to the new superintendent's office. I also asked that maintenance have the carpets cleaned, walls repainted, and his desk refinished before he arrived on the first day. When the new superintendent asked that I remain through the Baldrige site visit, I was pleased to do so.

It may sound like a lot of activities, but I remembered so well when I assumed command of new administrative offices, I was handed the keys and wished "good luck" by the leaving administrator. I didn't want that happening here, because sustaining the continuous improvement culture was so important.

Richard DeLorenzo; Chugach The Chugach School District continues to perform at high levels and is recognized as a leader throughout in educational innovations and excellence. The district continues to refine processes and look for new approaches that will have the greatest impact on students and teachers, but the most important development since 2001 has been the formation of ReInventing Schools Coalition (RISC), whose mission is to impact one million students or a thousand school districts by having them transition from a timed system to a highly accountable performance system that meets the needs of each child.

The district continues to refine processes and look for new approaches that will have the greatest impact on students and teachers, but the most important development since 2001 has been the formation of ReInventing Schools Coalition (RISC), whose mission is to impact one million students or a thousand school districts by having them transition from a timed system to a highly accountable performance system that meets the needs of each child.

Since its inception with the Chugach School District in 1994, the RISC model has been formalized and replicated in at least 15 districts and over 200 schools. The components of the model include leadership, shared vision, standards-based design, and continuous improvement—all components directly linked to the Baldrige Criteria. The validation of these processes has come from the Baldrige Criteria and several studies from various educational organizations and individual leaders including Dr. Robert Marzano.

Student results from coalition districts implementing the RISC model over four years are impressive, including double-digit gains in math and writing. (See reinventingschools.org for full report.)

> As far as I can tell, the RISC Model, as implemented by Chugach and other districts in Alaska involved with ReInventing Schools Coalition is the most comprehensive and well-articulated approach to standards-based reform in the entire country.
>
> —*Dr. Robert Marzano*

Joe Alexander; Monfort In our conversations with representatives from 2001 award recipient UW-Stout, we learned that, even now, organizations from across the U.S. and abroad continue to visit their campus and look to them as a role model. From a public relations standpoint, it certainly makes sense that these interactions are a healthy thing for one's organization. However, what UW-Stout shared with us, and something we have since found to be right on point, is that each individual you come into contact with has a story of his or her own to share. We continue making refinements in our performance excellence framework, and a number of those changes stem from best practices we have identified through interactions with those who were visiting to learn from us.

We continue making refinements in our performance excellence framework, and a number of those changes stem from best practices we have identified through interactions with those who were visiting to learn from us.

Having said that, looking back a couple of years, during the Baldrige site visit two of the examiners asked me, "How will your college keep the momentum of previous performance improvements going if you win or if you don't win?" As I attempted to share with them, at the time, our organization had already embraced the continuous improvement philosophy; it was part of our culture and rarely questioned by anyone in leadership.

As a result, even if we had not won that year, we were already observing so many significant changes in our results, it would have been foolish not to have continued our efforts to enhance our performance excellence framework.

Since we were fortunate enough to become a Baldrige recipient, I also think there is now some natural pressure, most of it self-induced, to continue justifying the trust placed in us by the entire Baldrige organization. In a true business sense, those performance results which offered sufficient evidence for us to win in 2004 are already dated at this point. So as I continue sharing our story with various audiences these days, one of the first questions they tend to ask is, "So, what have you done lately?" I think there is a natural curiosity to see if (1) maybe a recipient is a flash-in-the-pan for which all of the stars somehow aligned for one short time, or (2) a given recipient managed to somehow combine all of his or her energies into a sprint for the finish line in the organizational equivalent of a 100-meter dash.

For the most recent improvement cycle we achieved improvement on 15 of our 20 key performance indicators, with 4 indicators holding steady or exhibiting a one-cycle decline, and only 1 indicator showing a second consecutive year of decline. So, yes, we are continuing to improve in the majority of areas related to our student-centered process framework.

One additional observation worth noting in regards to where we are now positioned is that as we move closer to maximizing our potential scores on various key indicators, the potential gains become smaller (e.g., when you move from 86 percent to 97 percent customer satisfaction, the margin for additional improvement is obviously much smaller). Each year now, we have less total room to improve on our existing indicators. A portion of our planning sessions is now committed to prioritizing which indicators warrant further improvement in order to maximize the overall quality of our programs. This is turning out to be a very healthy experience in that it is forcing us

Each year now, we have less total room to improve on our existing indicators. A portion of our planning sessions is now committed to prioritizing which indicators warrant further improvement in order to maximize the overall quality of our programs. This is turning out to be a very healthy experience in that it is forcing us to take far more of a systems approach in our thinking than was occurring back in 2004.

to take far more of a systems approach in our thinking than was occurring back in 2004. I think the Baldrige community would view that as a natural part of the maturation process for an organization, and we still have a long ways to go.

Charles Sorensen; UW-Stout While closure to a project is generally viewed as an indicator of success, the Baldrige journey is one that requires continual attention and renewal. Becoming an award recipient is a major destination stop but only signals that the organization has demonstrated ability to maintain iterative processes and systems with proven outcomes. Changes in key personnel require continual team development, orientation to Baldrige Criteria, and monitoring by the leadership team. Continuing the momentum is hard work but allows an organization to remain competitive and provide value to the students, community, and economy.

Many organizations must also cope with post-award blues. This was the case at UW-Stout. We experienced a dip in overall morale, had initial difficulty in maintaining momentum in performance, and dealt with increasing expectations from stakeholders.

UW-Stout has experienced several post-award breakthroughs:

Agility: The university learned to take immediate action on our most important opportunities. Higher education has a reputation for long, drawn-out, committee-based, no-real-change actions. Applying for the Baldrige required that we demonstrate annual change and improvements, performance-based outcomes, and responsive initiatives. We have been able to maintain this momentum as we implement new initiatives such as our revamped first-year experience.

Comparative information: The university community has become much more adept at collecting, storing, retrieving, and utilizing data and information in a meaningful way. We are more engaged in national benchmarking opportunities such as the National Study of Student Engagement (NSSE) and its companion studies FSSE and BCSSE. We participate in the APPA, EDUCAUSE, NACUBO, and other professional organization benchmarking surveys because the data are useful in determining best practices and efficiency benchmarks. These results are shared widely on campus to encourage efforts at all levels of the organization to improve performance.

Validation: Receiving the Baldrige Award validates good practices and sound values. This by itself empowers members of the university community to continue with process improvements. As a result there is deeper penetration of planning systems within divisions and departments, improvements are proposed using data and benchmarking, and employees have a greater acceptance for accountability of projects and the resultant outcomes.

Learning environment: The most substantive change has been the interest by faculty and instructional staff to examine the teaching and learning environment to improve student learning outcomes. As we implemented the e-Scholar initiative, administrators and faculty worked together to design indicators to determine if learning outcomes were affected. Faculty demonstrated interest for a teaching and learning lab to experiment and share successes in integrating the laptop into the classroom experience. More recent initiatives include math and writing labs to improve student retention. These labs were designed after best-practice examples found nationally.

These labs have had a significant impact on student learning. For example, in the past two years, the center has served over 1200 students, achieving a 61 percent reduction in failure and withdrawal rates in Beginning Algebra and 23 percent in Intermediate Algebra. Figure 28 shows the percentage of students who failed or dropped out of Beginning Algebra (Math 010) from before until after the Math Teaching and Learning Center was initiated.

Faculty members are currently participating in the polytechnic initiative to research characteristics of polytechnic institutions that are appropriate and achievable at UW-Stout.

In general, the employees of our organization are actively involved in the work of the institution, are interested in professional development and opportunities for growth, remain innovative and entrepreneurial, and remain focused on a learner-centered environment.

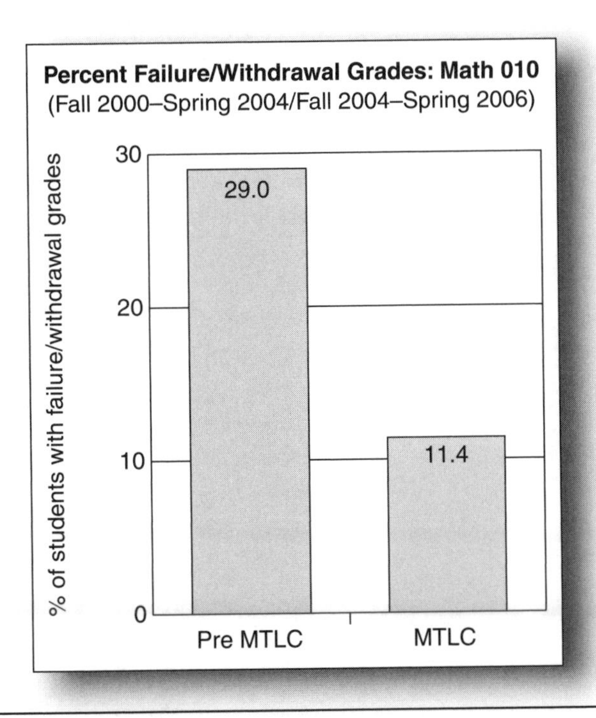

Figure 28 Math Center improved student retention.

Source: Math Teaching and Learning Center.

Conclusion

You've just had the unique opportunity to "listen" to a frank discussion from seven education leaders who stand apart from their peers, representing the only organizations to receive the prestigious Baldrige Award in Education. It's a rare occurrence; in fact, it's never before happened that all the education winners shared their experiences in one arena. The American Society for Quality is proud that it has been able to bring these leaders together in the hopes that their messages will inspire others and help pave the way for expanding the number of K–20 institutions dedicated to performance excellence using the "gold standard" Baldrige framework.

What you haven't had the opportunity to hear are the voices of the leadership teams from each institution. These are the people who provided support, helped with data analysis and the development of strategies, and rallied the employees to action throughout the journey to excellence. Our senior leaders tip their hats to those who stood beside them, not behind them, along the journey.

Just what can be gained from the words of these CEOs? After all, at first blush there doesn't seem to be much consistency in approach or views. You may be wondering, "What's 'best practice'? There seem to be so many approaches." This is precisely what defines the Baldrige process. It is a nonprescriptive approach to organizational excellence that recognizes the uniqueness of each organization. The Criteria allow any organization to frame its responses in terms of its own circumstances, vision, mission, and strategic challenges. At the same time, the Criteria are based on a set of research-based core values (see Appendix C) that, when attended to, provide the foundation for performance excellence. The goal (excellence) remains the same for all: to continuously improve the effectiveness and efficiency of key processes and align and integrate the system as a whole to improve student achievement.

While each of our CEOs has faced somewhat different challenges, a careful reading reveals some common threads. First, leaders set the vision. They must have the passion and belief that "it can happen," and then they work steadfastly to gain the support and trust of employees and key stakeholders. When critics or potential saboteurs bubble up, leaders open opportunities for them to become engaged.

Second, leaders must maintain constancy of purpose and stay the course, aligning mission with vision and establishing strategic goals based on key challenges. Then, they must align the budget to support change approaches and create a measurement system with leading indicators to allow everyone to understand whether the strategies are working. The CEOs all agree that without the use of data to regularly monitor progress toward the goal, there is no way to understand *what* needs to change.

Our leaders also spoke eloquently about that which most impacted the organization's Baldrige journey. Several specifically spoke about the value of developing relationships with award-winning business executives. The learning opportunities and mentoring they received enabled a personal learning curve that otherwise may have taken years to reach. This is one example of how education leaders may listen, learn, and even benchmark organizations outside the educational realm.

Two of our CEOs spoke of the importance of helping to establish a consortium of like-minded educators to help keep the momentum going and also to serve as a key listening and learning post for employees. Richard DeLorenzo (Chugach) spoke of creating the ReInventing Schools Coalition (RISC), and Richard Maurer (Pearl River) helped establish the Tristates Curriculum Consortium. John Conyers (CCSD15) was also instrumental in establishing an area consortium where best practices were shared. Likewise, Steve Mittlestet (Richland) joined the Continuous Quality Improvement Network and the League for Innovation in the Community College. Dr. Robert Marzano, one of the nation's experts on the transformation of education, said of RISC, "As far as I can tell, the RISC Model as implemented by Chugach and other districts in Alaska involved with ReInventing Schools Coalition is the most comprehensive and well-articulated approach to standards-based reform in the entire country."

Along these same lines, our higher education winners also spoke of benchmarking other institutions, even those with different missions. This common thread could be considered "best practice." The lesson is to establish a partnership with other excellent visionary CEOs and join a consortium of educational leaders aiming for excellence. If one does not exist, become a change agent and start one with schools or colleges within your region. The valuable lessons learned cannot be underestimated or dismissed by others seeking excellence.

Several of our leaders, even those who did not do so initially, shared the need to engage union leadership early in the journey. Most people have a natural desire to be included in the decision-making process, especially as it may affect their work and working relationships, system expectations, and benefits. John Conyers (District 15) and Kirby Lehman (Jenks) had to overcome the mistake of not involving the unions in the discussions and process as the Baldrige journey began—a mistake that resulted in longer buy-in time and consumed more energy to counteract the naysayers. This reality should strike a cord with every education CEO working in a collective bargaining unit state. As a key stakeholder group, unions are positioned to be strong supporters—or "foot-draggers." The bottom line is that all stakeholders need to be on board for the organization to stay the course. As Dr. John Conyers learned, you cannot ignore, overlook, or discount the influence of this group.

The CEOs had some differing opinions about how to start the journey, yet on closer examination there were many commonalities. For example, the leaders articulated a vision for excellence first and maintained a firm resolve and passionate belief that it was possible and necessary. What's interesting is that each of our CEOs came to the Baldrige starting line for a different reason: Richland College faced a crisis of state funding; Chugach had too many students not learning at adequate rates; Monfort decided to change its focus and offer only undergraduate programs in order to meet a void on the national business college landscape; and UW-Stout faced a campus crisis that questioned leadership decision making.

Whatever your circumstances, you will need passion and a steadfast determination coupled with courage to stay the course. You may decide to begin the journey by rallying the support of your board, the senior leadership team, or middle managers and teachers. Our leaders provided a rationale for the board (likening Baldrige to an external audit), trained the leadership team, and in several cases "disguised" Baldrige by calling the journey *continuous improvement* to avoid turning off people who, not understanding the Baldrige Criteria, initially may liken it to the management flavor of the month.

Other approaches used as a starting point for the Baldrige journey varied. For example, Charles Sorensen (UW-Stout) hired a former graduate and Baldrige examiner as a consultant to explain the Criteria and the data requirements. Others also used consultants to explain the process and to help solve problems by developing process maps or flowcharts or to help address specific challenges. The importance of celebrating early victories added to general buy-in among stakeholders and employees. Some of our CEOs became members of the Baldrige Board of Examiners and expected their leadership teams to assume this role too. The lesson learned is that the depth of understanding of the Criteria deepens when one becomes an examiner. Also, and perhaps as important, is that examiners are expected to evaluate at least one organization and in so doing return to their home organizations with insight into the gaps in their own system that otherwise may have gone unnoticed until much later in the journey.

Assigning Criteria champions was another common approach used by most of these CEOs. This approach allows members of the leadership team to become experts in one part of the Criteria, working with a team to engage in deep data analysis and process effectiveness and efficiency. It also provides a means for everyone to understand the interdependencies of each subsystem. Joe Alexander, from Monfort, described his experience of taking a Saturday phone call from someone in the admissions office who wanted to continue meetings with him because of a feeling that both entities benefited from the knowledge gained from such discussions. In other words, understanding how subsystems are interdependent on each other allows both to improve.

Our leaders agree that it is the journey—the process, the commitment to continuous improvement—that is the goal, *not* winning the award. All acknowledge the excellent public relations benefits and admitted to enjoying the *glow* that comes from being nationally recognized for excellence. However, they are all in agreement that whatever defines excellence at the time becomes outdated as time goes on. Joe Alexander (Monfort) was right when he said continuous improvement gets more difficult as the current processes function at or nearly at 100 percent effectiveness and efficiency. He goes on to say that this scenario means new processes must be designed in order to meet changing customer demands and to manage with a focus on the future if the organization is going to maintain the mantel of excellence. Continuous improvement, never letting your guard down, and keeping all employees motivated to meet the needs of customers and key stakeholders are the challenges that define organizations of today and the future.

Has Baldrige impacted the bottom line of the winning organizations? You bet! Examples abound and are as diverse as reduced costs of worker compensation, reductions in employee attrition, savings on paper costs and food services, and large increases in financial donations. But beyond this, and more importantly, the bottom line for education is improved student learning results, job placement rates, and student and stakeholder satisfaction rates. These results contributed in a major way to each of these organizations receiving the Baldrige Award.

Where are the CEOs now? Several have retired or moved on to new challenges. All remain dedicated to excellence and continue to share their stories with those who desire to learn. We appreciate that these outstanding leaders agreed to become contributors to this book. We hope you have enjoyed their stories as much as we have enjoyed listening and learning from them. Further, it is our hope that the attached CD with the Baldrige applications for each of these institutions, as well as the resources listed, will provide you with additional guidance for your journey.

If you have picked up and read this book, we know you are interested in improving education at your institution. This gives us all hope for the future of education and for the future of the next generation of Americans. Good luck on your journey.

Appendix A

Education Leaders' Biographies

Joe F. Alexander

Dean, Monfort College of Business at the University of Northern Colorado

Joe started at Monfort in 1990 as an assistant professor and was appointed associate dean in 1994. He served in that capacity for seven years before being appointed dean in 2002. As part of his initial goals, the administrative team was looking for a "stretch" goal to challenge employees and stakeholders as well as unite toward a common cause. The team decided that implementing the Baldrige Criteria with a goal of applying for and winning the award would be the best way to keep the college moving forward and improving. The college began a full-scale effort soon after Joe's appointment.

Monfort applied at the state level (Colorado Performance Excellence) and national level in March and April 2003, respectively. The leadership team determined that it could maximize the rate of improvement by applying for both simultaneously. There was about a two-month gap between the two application cycles, so the state application process was used as one improvement cycle with immediate improvements to hone the national application.

The college faced significant challenges, such as a 10 percent budget cut, during Joe's first two months as dean. At the time, this was viewed as a major obstacle, but Joe believes that the challenges of that financial environment pushed the college even harder to make the decisions needed to improve.

Joe has authored and co-authored a number of publications, including:

Alexander, J. F., J. Clinebell, S. Clinebell, T. Jares, C. Kelley, J. Kriss, M. Leonard, J. Lightfoot, R. Lynch, C. de la Torre, C. Cullom, R. Maddocks, and J. Burkey. 2006. "Monfort College of Business 2004 Baldrige National Quality Award Winner," ed. Laurence R. Smith. *Journal of Innovative Management* 10 (4): 7–38.

Jares, T. E., and J. Alexander. 2006. "Pursuing a Quality-Based Strategy: A Case Study of the First Business School to Earn the Baldrige Award." In K. D. Martell and T. G. Calderon, eds. *AACSB/AIR Assessment in Business Schools*. Tallahassee, FL: Association for Institutional Research.

Alexander, J. F. 2005. "The Power of Focus." AACSB International's *eNewsline* 4 (10): 2–3.

Joe received a DBA in Marketing from the University of Memphis in 1988, an MBA in Marketing from the same university in 1982, and a BBA in Marketing from Harding University in 1981.

Contact:
Monfort College of Business at the University of Northern Colorado
Campus Box 128, Greeley, CO 80639
970-351-2764
Fax: 970-351-2500
E-mail: joe.alexander@unco.edu

John G. Conyers

Educational Consultant and Executive Coach; formerly Superintendent, Community Consolidated School District 15 in 2003 when it received the Malcolm Baldrige National Quality Award

John has over 30 years of experience in education, from teaching to serving as a superintendent. He started at Consolidated School District 15 in 1985 and was at the helm in 2003 when it received the Baldrige National Quality Award. He currently consults with public and private organizations and has given presentations on educational issues to numerous organizations throughout the United

States and abroad. He has served as a Malcolm Baldrige examiner and also as a senior examiner for the Lincoln Foundation for Business Excellence. He has done consulting and presentations for the Metropolitan Police-Scotland Yard and Fisons Pharmaceutical Company in England; Japan Educational Systems; schools in London and Northern Ireland; the American Society for Quality; IBM Global Education Solutions; Edunetics Technology Group in Israel; the Beverly Hills, California school district; and, most recently, for the Education Leadership Conference in Beijing and the Cayman Islands Department of Education as well as the education ministries of Singapore, Malaysia, and Japan.

John has edited, authored, co-authored, and researched a number of publications:

Conyers, John G., and Robert Ewy. 2004. *Charting Your Course: Lessons Learned During the Journey Toward Performance Excellence.* Milwaukee, WI: ASQ Quality Press.

Conyers, John G., with Toni Kappel and Joanne Rooney. 1999. "How Technology Can Transform a School." *Educational Leadership* (February): 82–85.

Conyers, John G. 2000. "When Status Quo Won't Do." *The School Administrator* 57 (6): 22–27.

Conyers, John G., with George Lingel & Robert Piekarski. 2000. "5-Year Budget Forecasting." *School Business Affairs* 66 (11): 19–21.

Conyers, John G., with W. Christine Rauscher, 2000/2001. "An Antarctic Adventure." *Educational Leadership* (December/January): 69–72.

Conyers, John G. 2004. "Thinking outside to Support Newcomers." *The School Administrator* (June): 18–21.

- *The Reading Teacher*
- *Early Years*
- *The Research Review*
- *Education*
- *The Journal of Staff Development*
- *The American School Board Journal*
- *The School Administrator*
- *Annual Review of Communications/National Engineering Consortium*
- *Prism*
- *Outcomes*
- *Educational Leadership*
- *Promoting Social and Emotional Learning, Guidelines for Educators*

John earned his EdD in Educational Administration and Supervision from Oklahoma State University in 1976, an MA in Educational Administration and Supervision from Wichita State University in 1970, and a BS in Education from Friends University in 1968.

Contact:
Conyers JJ & Associates
1935 S. Plum Grove Road
Palatine, IL 60067
847-894-3677
E-mail: conyersjj@bellsouth.net

Richard DeLorenzo

Educational Specialist, ReInventing Schools Coalition (RISC); formerly Superintendent, Chugach Schools in 2001 when it received the Malcolm Baldrige National Quality Award

Richard assumed leadership responsibility at Chugach in 1994. A year later he started to implement the Baldrige Criteria as a management framework—before educational institutions were eligible for the award. When Chugach applied for the award in 2001, Alaska had no state award program. Chugach applied at the national level—and won—its first time out. As a result of the Chugach experience, Richard and others created the ReInventing Schools Coalition (RISC), with a mission to impact one million students in a thousand districts nationwide.

Richard has written and contributed to a number of publications:

DeLorenzo, R., W. Battino, R. Schrieber, and B. Gaddy. Forthcoming. *The Educational Revolution; Time to Performance; the Chugach Story.*

Marzano, R. 2006. *Classroom Assessment and Grading that Work.* Alexandria, VA: Association for Supervision and Curriculum Development.

DeLorenzo, R. 2003. "All Means All." In Duffy, F. *Courage, Passion, and Vision: A Guide to Leading Systemic School Improvement.* Lanham, MD: Scarecrow Press.

DeLorenzo, R. 2003. "A Way Up North." *Education Week* XXII: 37.

Wagner, T. 2003. *Making the Grade: Reinventing America's Schools.* New York: Routledge.

DeLorenzo, R. 2002. "Chugach School District—2001 Malcolm Baldrige National Quality Award Case Study." *Journal of Innovative Management.* 8:1.

DeLorenzo, R. 2002. "Chugach School District—2001 Baldrige Award Winner Profile." *Quality Digest* 22:8.

DeLorenzo, R., with W. Battino and R. Schrieber. 2002. *Guide for Reinventing Schools.* Self-published.

Richard earned his superintendent credentials from the University of Alaska in 1995, an Educational Administration degree from the University of Alaska in 1983, a Master of Education from the same university in 1981, and a BA from Central Washington University in 1979.

Contact:
ReInventing Schools Coalition (RISC)
PMB #352
1830 East Parks Highway, Suite A-113
Wasilla, AK 99654
907-357-9080
Fax: 907-373-6557
E-mail: rdelorenzo@gci.net

Kirby A. Lehman

Superintendent of Schools, Jenks Public Schools

Kirby began his tenure as Jenks (Oklahoma) School District Superintendent in February 1990. In 1995, the continuous improvement philosophy took root in the Jenks schools, with an outside consultant introducing the concepts of TQM in a workshop that included all Jenks administrators. Two years later Kirby introduced the concept of a Continuous Improvement Leadership Team, a group of district administrators who help keep the entire district focused on continuous improvement and the use of Quality tools.

Shortly after educational institutions were offered the opportunity to apply for the Baldrige Award, the Jenks team began the process of comparing the district's policies, practices, and procedures with the Baldrige Criteria and benchmarking with several private schools from around the world. In 2004, the Jenks team determined that the Jenks School District would complete the Baldrige application process. The application was submitted in May 2005, and the site examination took place in October. In November 2005, the Jenks School

District was selected to receive the 2005 Malcolm Baldrige National Quality Award on its first application.

Kirby has published several articles during the past 20 years. The most recent, "Establishing a Framework for Quality," appeared in the September 2006 issue of *The School Administrator*.

Kirby earned an EdD at Indiana University in 1975, an MS at Butler University in 1971, and a BA at Purdue University in 1968.

Contact:
Jenks Public Schools
205 East B Street
Jenks, Oklahoma 74037-3905
918-299-4415, ext. 2201
Fax: 918-299-9197
E-mail: kal@jenksps.org

Richard Maurer

Superintendent of Schools, Ardsley Public Schools; formerly Superintendent, Pearl River Public Schools when it received the Baldrige Award in 2001

Richard became superintendent at Pearl River Public Schools in 1998 after the district had already become involved with the Baldrige process. Pearl River had won the New York State Governor's Award in 1992 and had submitted an application for the MBNQA education pilot in 1995. Richard's chief contribution to implementing the Baldrige process in the district was driving the Baldrige continuous improvement philosophy deep into the organization's operating processes. For example, under Richard's watch, a Plan-Do-Study-Act model was instituted. This A+ approach is used by teachers in the classroom. The district applied for the Baldrige Award in 2000 and again in 2001, when it was named recipient of the Malcolm Baldrige National Quality Award.

Richard co-authored a book on using the Baldrige Criteria in education:

Maurer, R., and S. Cokeley-Pedersen. 2004. *Malcolm and Me: How to Use the Baldrige Process to Improve Your School.* Lanham, MD: Scarecrow Education.

Richard earned his PhD in Counseling from Fordham University in 1982, his MA from St. John's University in 1973, and a BA from Maryknoll College in 1968.

Contact:
Ardsley Public Schools
500 Farm Road
Ardsley, NY 10502
914-693-6300, ext. 2200
Fax: 914-693-8340
E-mail: maurerr@ardsleyschools.org

Stephen K. Mittelstet

President, Richland College

Stephen assumed CEO responsibility for Richland College in 1979. Richland began using the Baldrige Criteria under Stephen's leadership in the mid-1990s and soon applied for the Texas Award for Performance Excellence for feedback. That initial application and feedback proved a milestone that encouraged the college to continue its journey to being named a Baldrige education recipient in 2005.

Stephen earned a PhD from the University of Texas in 1972 and a BA from McMurry University in 1967.

Contact:
Richland College
1505 Elm Street, #1104
Dallas, TX 75201
972-238-6364
Fax: 972-238-6957
E-mail: stevem@dcccd.edu

Charles W. Sorensen

Chancellor, University of Wisconsin-Stout

Charles arrived at UW-Stout in 1988. Some basic TQM processes were implemented in the early 1990s and the institution spent several years on them, bringing in outside consultants and organizing TQM teams with assigned projects. This worked in some areas, but for the most part the effort was unsuccessful and was quietly dropped. The Baldrige process was evaluated in 1999, the year that the award was expanded to include education. Charles had served as chancellor for 11 years by then and saw the real need for a systematic, strategic look at the university. He became an early and strong supporter of the effort to use the Baldrige process because it was so thorough and provided such insight to the organization.

The decision to apply for the Malcolm Baldrige National Quality Award had its roots in a campus crisis that led to a vote of no confidence against Charles. At issue was whether UW-Stout should become a charter school, withdraw from the University of Wisconsin System, and assume the role as a state-supported, independent state university. The idea was encouraged by the UW System to see if such an organization could deliver programs more effectively, raise more extramural funds, and be more responsive to stakeholder needs. This experimental idea had strong support from the UW System, the board of regents, and even the governor. But some faculty members voiced very strong opposition to the idea. The issue had not been well communicated and the campus felt betrayed; a major crisis developed that lasted nearly six months.

Charles chose to react in a positive way to recover the trust essential to managing a campus. He listened to all of the concerns intently for six months and then implemented four changes that were essential to regain trust: the creation of a Chancellor's Advisory Council representing all constituents on campus so all groups could be influential in decision making; the creation of an office of Budget, Planning, and Analysis, assuming a CFO function; the appointment of a chief information officer; and the development of an open, democratic planning process.

With these in place by the fall of 1996, the university was able to begin rebuilding trust and applied for and won the Baldrige Award in 2001.

Charles has authored and co-authored a number of publications:

Sorensen, C. W. 2006. "Interview Best Business Practices." *Journal of Communications Technology in Higher Education* (Spring): 27-30.

Sorensen, C., J. Furst-Bowe, and D. Moen, eds. 2005. *Quality and Performance Excellence in Higher Education: Baldrige on Campus*. Bolton, MA: Anker Publishing.

Sorensen, C. 2004. "From Crisis to Malcolm Baldrige National Quality Award Winner: Transforming the University of Wisconsin-Stout with a Grassroots Strategic Planning Process." *Higher Education Digest: Insights for College and University Leaders* (October), http://www.internetviz-newsletters.com/datatel/e_article000220001.cfm?X=b3MtDgh,blk.

Sorensen, C. 2003. "From Crisis to Malcolm Baldrige National Quality Award." *New York Times*, September 7. http://www.nytimes.com/college/collegespecial4/index.html.

Sorensen, C. 2003. "University of Wisconsin-Stout; 2001 Malcolm Baldrige National Quality Award." *Journal of Innovative Management* (Winter): 41–78.

Sorensen, C. 2002. "2001 Baldrige Award Winner Profile." *Quality Digest* (September): 51–53.

Charles earned a PhD in American History from Michigan State University in 1973, an MS from Illinois State University in 1967, and an AB from Augustana College in 1965.

Contact:
University of Wisconsin-Stout
712 South Broadway, Administration Building
Menomonie, WI 54751
715-232-2441
Fax: 715-232-1416
E-mail: sorensenc@uwstout.edu

Appendix B

Summary of Dr. Michael T. Noble's Case Study Review of Baldrige in Education School Districts 2005, Including the First Three Baldrige in Education Winners

Dr. Michael T. Noble's case study documents the evolution and performance of the first three K–12 Baldrige in Education (BiE) Award winners: Chugach, Alaska; Pearl River, New York; and Community Consolidated School District 15, Palatine, Illinois; and two other California schools that had at least three years' experience implementing BiE at the time of the study. The California schools are Miramonte Elementary School in the Clovis Unified School District and Hill Classical Middle School in the Long Beach Unified School District.

The study documents the processes used to establish school reform efforts and to measure performance and outcomes by the schools using the BiE process, including the metrics they used to periodically evaluate or oversee their performance. Dr. Noble's research also describes the decision-making and change management process used to transform the organization from a traditional school model to the BiE model. His research discusses how these schools identified, added, or adapted educational standards or curricula; built capacity of employees; and developed individual student learning plans, including implementing learning or development activities. In addition, he explores the use of data portfolios, assignment rubrics, student learning profiles, individual learning plans, and benchmark testing or formative assessments.

In 2001, the Department of Commerce awarded Chugach, Alaska, and Pearl River, New York, with the first K–12 BiE Awards. This prestigious award was not awarded again until 2003, when Community Consolidated School District 15, Palatine, Illinois, received it.

The purpose of this study was to learn why schools adopted the BiE model, to learn how the BiE continuous improvement process was successfully established in schools, and to describe the common approaches used by these schools and identify those implementation designs that are different.

In addition, Dr. Noble's study documents the leadership roles played by key change agents, their process for understanding and meeting stakeholders' needs, and the outcomes achieved. It is important to know how the BiE continuous improvement initiatives performed in various schools and if stakeholder satisfaction and pupil performance improved because of them.

Four of the five school districts started looking at quality management systems in business before there was a BiE model. Long Beach was the only school to begin implementing a quality school model after the federal government established BiE in 1998. The other schools started by adapting the business model for their schools.

A critical factor observed by Dr. Noble that defines a school district's potential for success or failure when implementing a quality school model process is leadership. The leadership of schools included in this study believed they could and must do something different to improve instruction and meet student/stakeholder needs. The leadership teams believed the school districts could do things differently to improve their performance.

The leadership took a strong hand in managing the budget and cutting overhead costs and understood what was necessary to develop a shared vision to improve education in their districts and schools. The leadership teams made many changes and improved organizational and process efficiency while recognizing the importance of being relationship focused, involving stakeholders, and having clearly defined goals.

The senior leadership of the district led the journey, learning the continuous improvement process first. They modeled it for the staff and faculty by implementing the Plan-Do-Study-Act (PDSA) cycle to facilitate continuous improvement. Site administrators led their faculty and staff to use the PDSA process in their classrooms. They collected, evaluated, and prioritized data and reported the results of their data analysis back to their staff and stakeholders to reinforce their involvement in the BiE process and to share in its success.

However, other schools in the study approached the data challenge by using grade- and department-level collaborative teams of teachers to disaggregate data and to tailor individual student or group learning plans. All schools in the study created a clear, continuous formative assessment and performance-leveling process. They used rubrics and tried to build relevant thematic learning into their model. Students set and monitored their goals using individual student data portfolios and often tutored one another.

Chugach leadership believed that age-graded classrooms must be eliminated if schools are going to be successful in meeting the challenges of NCLB.

As an example, they believe that in a class of fourth graders it is unlikely that all the students are at the same instructional level in all subject areas. Therefore, how do you teach those diverse populations of students at different instructional levels? If your teaching is not at their level, then it is going to either frustrate or bore them. Therefore, Chugach created a system that serves students at their individual developmental level.

The districts involved stakeholders in their strategic planning process. After adopting their strategic plan, the districts aligned all their operations to better support their mission and vision. The districts identified what they needed to do to improve performance based on data and reallocated and prioritized their budgets. None of the districts received extra funding to implement the continuous improvement process.

Schools in the study shared a common vision that grew out of a belief that all children can and will learn. BiE schools saw their students as customers. Their focus was on the students and what they needed to have a great year and how the current year aligned with all other years in their K–12 education experience. They also focused on aligning building goals, department goals, and goals for the classroom. Schools in the study looked at education as a continuum from kindergarten to grade 12. They were no longer focused on single grades or a specific subject in the textbook. They listened to their teachers and worked in collaborative teams to clearly understand what their needs were.

The planning process occurred at three levels—district, building, and classroom—and focused on developing a shared vision with active involvement from all stakeholders, including faculty, staff, and district operations. Employees were considered essential in the design of their processes, which fostered maximum involvement of classroom teachers. The schools in the study also believed that every goal must have a measure.

Consolidated established BiE category champions, and Pearl River had section champions. These individual teams were responsible for planning and implementing each of the BiE categories and for providing the superintendent with periodic progress reports on the process.

Corporate partners encouraged schools in the study to implement BiE as a process for increasing accountability and their overall performance. Chugach and Consolidated appeared to have been the most focused and deliberate with regard to involving their communities in developing a shared vision. Chugach had a series of meetings with its villages for 12 to 18 months before implementing the continuous improvement process and empowered community leaders to facilitate the meetings to increase stakeholder ownership. To ensure community involvement, Consolidated set up its District Advisory Committee for Educational Excellence (DACEE) with more than 60 members, including businesses, elected officials, and PTA representatives.

The quality school process began with discussions with "customers" (or stakeholders), the parents and community, local businesses, and the students themselves to identify their needs and goals. This was at the heart of the process for creating a shared vision with stakeholders.

The other districts involved community representatives but not to the same degree as Chugach and Consolidated. As an example, parents in Long Beach were exposed to the continuous improvement process, including the use of tools, to invite their input. They had received feedback from the schools and saw the improvements in the schools, but they had not been involved in the detailed planning and community meetings that Chugach and Consolidated used in their planning and continuous improvement processes.

The administration and building leadership teams held meetings with parents and teachers, treating them as partners to collaboratively look at what was needed to improve performance. Stakeholder involvement and feedback were important to all districts in the study. The process of valuing or honoring stakeholders' needs was a critical part of the successful BiE model. All schools in the study believed one must have a shared vision and involve people in the process to get their understanding and buy-in. Schools believed that stakeholders needed to understand what they were trying to accomplish, and the administration needed to enroll the community members and businesses.

Pearl River and Consolidated committed resources specifically to communications by hiring communications and public relations directors. Consolidated also hired a planning director to help the superintendent coordinate and carry out the district-level planning process and to ensure that all school-level plans were aligned with the district's goals and mission. Another unique and specific tool used only by Consolidated was the Web-based One-Page Planning process that helped promote the alignment and accountability of progress-tracking processes.

Consolidated also had its leadership team actively take part in various community groups such as the Rotary Club and the Chamber of Commerce, while other districts left this level of community involvement to the superintendent. In addition, Consolidated's communications director produced two newsletters for its schools each year. The content in the four-page newsletter was split between the school and the district and used for stakeholder feedback.

All the districts used the PDSA cycle as part of their implementation and continuous improvement process and ensured that stakeholders' concerns or recommendations were recognized. If a recommendation could not be carried out, they explained why. All districts stressed the importance of preserving a high level of communications and feedback with stakeholders.

BiE schools said they strategically used community/stakeholder input and reflected what they believed stakeholders said so they could see that their thoughts and concerns were being considered. Deputy Superintendent Bob Crumley in Chugach said that if one does not act on stakeholders' input, his or her trust is lost, and those stakeholders may not be back for the next meeting.

All schools in the study conducted staff, community, parent, teacher, and student surveys and focus groups. The stakeholder input was used to develop a shared vision and ensure involvement in the continuous improvement process. Employee satisfaction surveys were also conducted and shared with the school as part of the continuous improvement process. The surveys' data and stakeholder input were used to create and continuously update action plans and provide stakeholder feedback so stakeholders knew their concerns were being addressed.

Teachers developed goals, and rather than working independently, they worked in collaborative teams adjusting instructional strategies on the basis of formative assessment feedback. District leaders also set strategic objectives on the basis of student and stakeholder needs identified through assessments. Schools in the study defined metrics and established leading and lagging indicators or goals to monitor progress on their action plans. The continuous improvement process gave students ownership in the system, and implementing Baldrige provided schools with data-rich processes and ways to use the data to help improve academic performance.

Consolidated did not want to be data rich and information poor; therefore, its balanced scorecard data were collected and provided to leadership using the district's education data warehouse (EDW). Chugach developed a similar program (AIMs), and Clovis used a commercial program, Edusoft, to supplement its data management systems with Edusoft's formative tests and test data disaggregation capabilities. The systems allowed users to work with many variables, including factors like socioeconomic status, nationality, grade level, subject, and attendance.

The data-driven approach used by the schools in the study contributed to a reflective process, which made change a part of the district's culture. It was part of their system. As an example, teachers disaggregated test data using item analysis techniques and worked in collaborative teams. Teachers were willing to share their analysis, which happened because of trust. If the staff did not trust one another and the system, they would not have been willing to do this, according to the administrators interviewed.

Administrators led their faculty and staff to use the PDSA process in their classrooms. They collected, evaluated, and prioritized data and often reported the results of their data analysis back to their staff and stakeholders to reinforce their involvement in the process and to share in their success.

Significant organizational improvement occurred because the schools focused on management by fact and sharing data analysis. Continuous improvement and the PDSA cycle needed solid data so the district could make informed decisions. All the schools in the study used data binders. The student portfolios defined where each student was and what he or she needed to do to close the achievement gap. If a child was struggling, the schools would develop an individual learning plan and IDP. (Note that Chugach used IDPs for every student.) All the departments did surveys, including random spot-checks and surveys between the larger reviews and focus group meetings.

The PDSA cycle was key to implementing change, and people who were not familiar with this as part of the continuous improvement process found change to be more difficult. Quality improvement teams (QITs) were also used for specific targeted areas of improvement. District in-service training was designed to promote change management, share lessons learned in implementing the continuous improvement process, and encourage the use of the student data portfolios.

Schools in the study believed the continuous improvement process did not cost anything. When setting up BiE they did not do anything that was not required; they just started doing it differently. There was no extra funding in the beginning for any of the schools in the study.

All schools in the study used formative assessments to lead instruction. In addition, Chugach evaluated every student's learning style or profile and included this understanding when working with him or her to develop learning plans and when assigning projects.

Unlike many California districts, Clovis has continued to provide resources for the performing arts, athletics, counseling, nursing services, psychological services, primary (K–3) and ninth-grade class-size reduction, students with exceptional educational needs, and student transportation. Clovis believes these are all vital to student success and necessary to ensure their students are the best they can be in mind, body, and spirit.

A key element in improving student learning and involving students in their learning process was the use of the student data portfolio, goal setting, and the IDP. Students owned their plans and took a leadership role in managing their progress and tracking performance in their student data portfolios. The teacher and student identified student strengths and weaknesses and developed the student-driven plan. The portfolios included goals, action steps, and aligned assessments put together by each student in collaboration with teachers and parents.

BiE helped create a positive process where stakeholders wanted to work together. Classrooms developed mission statements, and students were engaged in planning their education using their student data portfolios to establish goals and monitor their progress.

Classrooms worked in collaborative groups to help each student achieve individual and class goals. The PDSA charts and various other tools helped the class stay focused on its goal of highest possible achievement. According to the teachers interviewed, Baldrige classrooms had fewer discipline problems because students knew what was expected of them and they had participated in setting up the classroom norms, mission, and goals.

In 2005, Roger Sampson, Alaska's Commissioner of Education said it was important to have a standard that measured across multiple content areas because that reflected real life; that is what was expected. "One is not going to be learning grammar just for the sake of knowing grammar. One needs to be able to apply what is learned in the language arts and grammar to history, science, and eventually to jobs."

All three of the Baldrige Award–winning school districts believed that successful organizations must engage in benchmarking to understand the world-class performance of similar organizations or their competitors' plans for achieving breakthrough performance. Benchmarks show comparative data against which to measure an organization's performance. Benchmarking meant the districts identified the best-in-class in areas where they wanted to improve their performance. They did not compare themselves with or target average performers.

Chugach, Pearl River, and Consolidated all benchmarked and compared their performance with the best because the districts did not want to be average. Their goals were to be as good as or better than the best academically and in all operational performance areas.

Districts also needed to measure "little bites" of how well the students were doing so the districts could use the information to make a difference in performance. Sampson saw the lack of an effective formative assessment process as one of the single largest things that have been missing with all states in their assessment process. Because assessments must be aligned to curriculum and standards, the use of scoring guides or rubrics was a key component of the grading mechanism for assessments and was seen as a critical component of the curriculum or learning plans.

The scoring guide was a powerful process that served as both a teaching tool and an assessment tool. Scoring guides could be regarded as the link between school/district standards, instruction, and assessment of each individual student. They complemented any lesson, performance task, thematic unit, or real life for both instruction and assessment. Because more than one standard could be evaluated at the same time, scoring guides were often custom developed for each activity. The use of rubrics or scoring guides often created multiple forms of student assessment.

Like Chugach and Consolidated, Clovis rewrote state standards so they were more student and parent friendly. The Clovis standards were a tool that students could use to develop their goals and objectives. Consolidated developed these parent- and student-friendly standards and referred to them as learning statements, which were posted in each classroom.

SUMMARY OF KEY FINDINGS

Powerful outcomes or results of BiE in the studied schools include:

- Dramatic improvement in academic performance over a three- to five-year period
- Increased student motivation and sense of ownership for their education
- Increased and positive community/stakeholder involvement in education; schools understood their stakeholders' needs, using the continuous improvement cycle and stakeholder surveys
- Use of student data portfolios, IDPs, and student learning profiles (SLPs) to help define and manage student-owned learning plans
- Use of professional learning communities or grade/department-level collaboration teams to disaggregate data and support team performance improvement

- Use of rubrics, scoring guides, and formative-benchmark assessments to inform instruction and help students monitor their progress
- Understanding and use of the PDSA cycle and classroom quality tools
- Use of student peer coaching and mentoring

CONCLUSIONS

> Baldrige, unlike many other strategies, is nonprescriptive. The process empowers people—parents, teachers, administrators, school board members, business people and students themselves—to influence, control, and act positively. It creates ownership. It enables people to work as partners to set common goals. The BiE process yields results in terms of student achievement and behavior. Students come to understand and value their opportunity to learn.

The results of Dr. Noble's study support many of the education reforms discussed earlier in this chapter and include:

1. Strong school leadership is critical for the success of BiE. Overall, implementation of the BiE process, the leadership style, and the courage to stay the course resulted in positive and significant academic and operational performance improvement with these schools. All the successful schools had strong leadership support from the superintendent. School leadership identified and involved all stakeholders in the education process, including students, parents, teachers, businesses, and the community, to develop a shared vision and ensure good continuing communications with these groups. None of the schools had extra funds to set up BiE in the beginning; however, four of them were awarded grants from various organizations, including the federal government, after implementing the process. By reallocating their existing budgets, school leadership was able to get started with the process. However, with shrinking budgets they all found it difficult to provide an appropriate level of training and coaching for their teachers without extra funding.
2. Schools need to teach students to develop learning plans that align with their individual goals, and action plans that include coaching, feedback, and teamwork. Students must understand the ILPs as a process. Student and teacher coaching and facilitation must also be available to ensure student success and the success of the teacher's collaborative teams.

   Students must be involved with the process, including defining goals and action plans and continuously monitoring their progress in their student data portfolios. Some schools also encouraged student cross-age tutoring and mentoring. More thematic learning and relevant cross-content projects should be part of each school, grade, and classroom plan, including assigning students to work collaboratively on projects. The Chugach Balanced Instruction Model is the best example of how this concept could be implemented.

3. We need to teach students and support learning at the student's individual and developmentally appropriate level versus age-graded classrooms. Students of the same age are not equal, and some experts recommend reversing time as a constant and learning as a variable in our classrooms, stating that learning should be the constant and time the variable for each content or subject area and student. Chugach has made tremendous progress eliminating age-graded classrooms, and Marzano (2003) states the Chugach standards-based model is the best he has seen.

4. Teachers must work in collaborative teams to clarify standards, define common assignments/projects, develop and/or ensure that department- and grade-level teacher teams are using common assignment and project rubrics, and conduct frequent in-process reviews using formative or benchmark assessments. Teachers must also focus on student learning versus teaching as a goal and work in collaborative teams with other grade- and department-level teachers to disaggregate test data and analyze assessment findings using the derived information in a much more proactive, diagnostic, and prescriptive way. In addition, schools should assign the best teachers to the most difficult students.

5. Schools must use the 80:20 or Pareto Principle to get noncritical activities off the teachers' plates and to focus on those critical goals and activities that will make a great difference in student learning. Schools need to rationalize standards and recast critical standards in teacher-, student-, and parent-friendly terms with equally clear goals that both the teacher and the student teams can understand and embrace as part of the student's ILP.

6. We must have board members who are working to support the best interests of students and education and not special interest groups or individual political goals. Board members must understand the quality and team approaches to education and ensure that they align their policy direction with these initiatives.

7. The schools in this study benchmarked performance against best performers and not against average performers, which helps them to produce increasingly positive performance results.

8. All the schools included in Dr. Noble's study took advantage of technology. They used data management systems to administer formative tests and to simplify data disaggregation at the grade or department level, thus encouraging the use of collaborative teams to help improve

education. Schools must invest more in technology to effectively deliver curriculum and assessments; to share information; to provide for longitudinal progress of individual students, teachers, and schools; and to be connected to our global community.

FINAL REMARKS

The Quality Schools Model or BiE creates an excellent framework for aligning education reform in any school district, as evident with the results of the schools included in Dr. Noble's study. The results of this research confirm the need for more research and for implementing significant changes in how we currently approach education.

Eliminating the agrarian education model and the age-graded classroom is the key to any serious effort to reform education and not leave any child behind. Teacher collaboration and eliminating teachers' working independently, use of frequent benchmark assessments, and changing the NCLB assessment process must all be part of future national policy change efforts to reform public education.

Schools in the study effectively used formative assessments to monitor their performance and the performance of individual students. Summative testing as it is administered today for NCLB contributes very little to inform learning at the individual student or classroom level. NCLB is well intended but poorly designed from an assessment perspective. The following changes must be made to have an accountability system that works while contributing to student learning and progress in our schools:

- All states should administer the same summative tests
- Each school, school district, and state department of education should administer standards-based formative tests that drive curriculum, map out individual student's performance, and document school and student growth or progress

Annual yearly progress (AYP) reports should be based on data from a series of standards-based formative tests. The classroom teacher should administer the tests and the data combined with a shorter, perhaps multiple-choice, summative test to document individual student growth and school achievement. This approach would not only measure real progress but could also have a marked effect on informing individual student and classroom performance.

CURRICULUM VITAE

Dr. Noble's doctoral research evaluated education reform using BiE quality management systems.

Education

University of La Verne, La Verne, California—Doctorate in Organizational Leadership

Golden Gate University, San Francisco, California—Master of Business Administration in Health Care Administration

University of South Carolina, Columbia, South Carolina—Master of Science in Public and Environmental Health, Bachelor of Science in Biology

Publications

Noble, Michael T. 2000. *Organizational Mastery with Integrated Management Systems/Controlling the Dragon.* Hoboken, NJ: John Wiley & Sons.

Appendix C

2006 Education Criteria: Core Values, Concepts, and Framework

CRITERIA PURPOSES

The Criteria are the basis for conducting organizational self-assessments, for making Awards, and for giving feedback to applicants. In addition, the Criteria have three important roles:

- to help improve organizational performance practices, capabilities, and results
- to facilitate communication and sharing of best practices information among U.S. organizations of all types
- to serve as a working tool for understanding and managing performance and for guiding organizational planning and opportunities for learning

Education Criteria for Performance Excellence Goals

The Criteria are designed to help organizations use an integrated approach to organizational performance management that results in

- delivery of ever-improving value to students and stakeholders, contributing to education quality and organizational stability
- improvement of overall organizational effectiveness and capabilities
- organizational and personal learning

Source: NIST, Malcolm Baldrige National Quality Award Criteria for Performance Excellence, http://www.quality.nist.gov/Education_Criteria.htm

CORE VALUES AND CONCEPTS

The Criteria are built on the following set of interrelated Core Values and Concepts:

- visionary leadership
- learning-centered education
- organizational and personal learning
- valuing faculty, staff, and partners
- agility
- focus on the future
- managing for innovation
- management by fact
- social responsibility
- focus on results and creating value
- systems perspective

These values and concepts, described below, are embedded beliefs and behaviors found in high-performing organizations. They are the foundation for integrating key performance and operational requirements within a results-oriented framework that creates a basis for action and feedback.

Visionary Leadership

Your organization's senior leaders should set directions and create a student-focused, learning-oriented climate; clear and visible values; and high expectations. The directions, values, and expectations should balance the needs of all your stakeholders. Your leaders should ensure the creation of strategies, systems, and methods for achieving performance excellence, stimulating innovation, building knowledge and capabilities, and ensuring organizational sustainability. The values and strategies should help guide all of your organization's activities and decisions. Senior leaders should inspire and motivate your entire workforce and should encourage all faculty and staff to contribute, to develop and learn, to be innovative, and to be creative. Senior leaders should be responsible to your organization's governance body for their actions and performance. The governance body should be responsible ultimately to all your stakeholders for the ethics, actions, and performance of your organization and its senior leaders.

Senior leaders should serve as role models through their ethical behavior and their personal involvement in planning, communications, coaching, development of future leaders, review of organizational performance, and faculty and staff recognition. As role models, they can reinforce ethics, values, and expectations while building leadership, commitment, and initiative throughout your organization.

In addition to their important role within the organization, senior leaders have other avenues to strengthen education. Reinforcing the learning environment in the organization might require building community support and aligning community and business leaders and community services with this aim.

Learning-Centered Education

In order to develop the fullest potential of all students, education organizations need to afford them opportunities to pursue a variety of avenues to success. Learning-centered education supports this goal by placing the focus of education on learning and the real needs of students. Such needs derive from market and citizenship requirements.

A learning-centered organization needs to fully understand these requirements and translate them into appropriate curricula and developmental experiences. For example, changes in technology and in the national and world economies have increased demands on employees to become knowledge workers and problem solvers, keeping pace with the rapid market changes. Most analysts conclude that to prepare students for this work environment, education organizations of all types need to focus more on students' active learning and on the development of problem-solving skills. Educational offerings also need to be built around effective learning, and effective teaching needs to stress promotion of learning and achievement.

Learning-centered education is a strategic concept that demands constant sensitivity to changing and emerging student, stakeholder, and market requirements and to the factors that drive student learning, satisfaction, and persistence. It demands anticipation of changes in the education market. Therefore, learning-centered education demands awareness of developments in technology and competitors' programs and offerings, as well as rapid and flexible responses to student, stakeholder, and market changes.

Key characteristics of learning-centered education include the following:

- High developmental expectations and standards are set for all students.
- Faculty understand that students may learn in different ways and at different rates. Student learning rates and styles may differ over time and may vary depending on subject matter. Learning may be influenced by support, guidance, and climate factors, including factors that contribute to or impede learning. Thus, the learning-centered organization needs to maintain a constant search for alternative ways to enhance learning. Also, the organization needs to develop actionable information on individual students that affects their learning.

- A primary emphasis on active learning is provided. This may require the use of a wide range of techniques, materials, and experiences to engage student interest. Techniques, materials, and experiences may be drawn from external sources, such as businesses, community services, or social service organizations.
- Formative assessment is used to measure learning early in the learning process and to tailor learning experiences to individual needs and learning styles.
- Summative assessment is used to measure progress against key, relevant external standards and norms regarding what students should know and should be able to do.
- Students and families are assisted in using self-assessment to chart progress and to clarify goals and gaps.
- There is a focus on key transitions, such as school-to-school and school-to-work.

Organizational and Personal Learning

Achieving the highest levels of organizational performance requires a well-executed approach to organizational and personal learning. Organizational learning includes both continuous improvement of existing approaches and significant change, leading to new goals and approaches. Learning needs to be embedded in the way your organization operates. This means that learning (1) is a regular part of daily work; (2) is practiced at personal, work unit, department, and organizational levels; (3) results in solving problems at their source ("root cause"); (4) is focused on building and sharing knowledge throughout your organization; and (5) is driven by opportunities to effect significant, meaningful change. Sources for learning include ideas from faculty and staff, education and learning research findings, students' and stakeholders' input, best practice sharing, and benchmarking.

Improvement in education requires a strong emphasis on effective design of educational programs, curricula, and learning environments. The overall design should include clear learning objectives, taking into account the individual needs of students. Design also must include effective means for gauging student progress. A central requirement of effective design is the inclusion of an assessment strategy. This strategy needs to emphasize the acquisition of formative information—information that provides an early indication of whether or not learning is taking place—to minimize problems that might arise if learning barriers are not promptly identified and addressed.

Faculty and staff success depends increasingly on having opportunities for personal learning and practicing new skills. Organizations invest in personal learning through education, training, and other opportunities for continuing growth and development. Such opportunities might include job rotation and increased pay for demonstrated knowledge and skills. Education and training programs may benefit from technologies, such as computer- and Internet-based learning and satellite broadcasts.

Personal learning can result in (1) more satisfied and versatile faculty and staff who stay with your organization, (2) organizational cross-functional learning, (3) the building of your organization's knowledge assets, and (4) an improved environment for innovation.

Thus, learning is directed not only toward better educational programs and services but also toward being more adaptive, innovative, flexible, and responsive to the needs of students, stakeholders, and the market, as well as giving your faculty and staff satisfaction and motivation to excel.

Valuing Faculty, Staff, and Partners

An organization's success depends increasingly on the diverse backgrounds, knowledge, skills, creativity, and motivation of all its faculty, staff, and partners, including volunteers, as appropriate.

Valuing faculty and staff means committing to their satisfaction, development, and well-being. Increasingly, this involves more flexible, high-performance work practices tailored to faculty and staff with varying workplace and home life needs. For staff, development might include classroom and on-the-job training, job rotation, and pay for demonstrated skills. For faculty, development means building not only discipline knowledge but also knowledge of student learning styles and of assessment methods. Faculty participation might include contributing to the organization's policies and working in teams to develop and execute programs and curricula. Increasingly, participation is becoming more student-focused and more multidisciplinary. Organization leaders should work to eliminate disincentives for groups and individuals to sustain these important, learning-focused professional development activities.

Major challenges in the area of valuing faculty and staff include (1) demonstrating your leaders' commitment to the success of your faculty and staff, (2) providing recognition that goes beyond the regular compensation system, (3) ensuring development and progression within your organization, (4) sharing your organization's knowledge so your faculty and staff can better serve your students and stakeholders and contribute to achieving your strategic objectives, (5) creating an environment that encourages creativity and innovation, and (6) creating a supportive environment for a diverse workforce.

Education organizations need to build internal and external partnerships to better accomplish overall goals. Internal partnerships might include cooperation among senior leaders, faculty, and staff. Partnerships with faculty and staff might entail faculty and staff development, cross-training, or new organizational structures, such as high-performance work teams. Internal partnerships also might involve creating network relationships among your work units to improve flexibility, responsiveness, and knowledge sharing.

External partnerships might be with other schools, suppliers, businesses, business associations, and community and social service organizations—all stakeholders and potential contributors. Strategic partnerships or alliances are increasingly important kinds of external partnerships. Such partnerships might offer entry into new markets or a basis for new programs or services. Also, partnerships might permit the blending of your organization's core competencies or leadership capabilities with the complementary strengths and capabilities of partners to address common issues.

Successful internal and external partnerships develop longer-term objectives, thereby creating a basis for mutual investment and respect. Partners should address the key requirements for success, means for regular communication, approaches to evaluating progress, and means for adapting to changing conditions. In some cases, joint education and training could offer a cost-effective method for employee development.

Agility

Success in today's ever-changing, globally competitive environment demands agility—a capacity for faster and more flexible responses to the needs of your students and stakeholders. Many organizations are learning that an explicit focus on and measurement of response times help drive the simplification of the organizational structure and work processes. Education organizations are increasingly being asked to respond rapidly to new or emerging social issues. Empowered faculty and staff are vital assets in responding to today's changing and demanding environment.

All aspects of time performance are becoming increasingly important and should be among your key process measures. Other important benefits can be derived from this focus on time; time improvements often drive simultaneous improvements in organization, quality, and cost.

Focus on the Future

In today's education environment, creating a sustainable organization requires understanding the short- and longer-term factors that affect your organization and the education market. Pursuit of education excellence requires a strong future orientation and a willingness to make long-term commitments to students and key stakeholders—your community, parents, employers, faculty and staff, suppliers, partners, and the public.

Your organization's planning should anticipate many factors, such as changes in educational requirements and instructional approaches, resource availability, students' and stakeholders' expectations, new partnering opportunities, faculty and staff development and hiring needs, technological developments, the evolving Internet environment, changes in demographics and in student and market segments, changes in community and societal expectations and needs, and strategic moves by comparable organizations. Strategic objectives and resource allocations need to accommodate these influences. A major longer-term investment associated with your organization's improvement is the investment in creating and sustaining a mission-oriented assessment system focused on learning. This entails faculty education and training in assessment methods. In addition, the organization's leaders should be familiar with research findings and practical applications of assessment methods and learning style information. A focus on the future includes developing faculty and staff, accomplishing effective succession planning, creating opportunities for innovation, and anticipating public responsibilities and concerns.

Managing for Innovation

Innovation means making meaningful change to improve an organization's programs, services, processes, and operations and to create new value for the organization's stakeholders. Innovation should lead your organization to new dimensions of performance. Innovation is no longer strictly the purview of research; innovation is important for providing ever-improving educational value to students and for improving all educational and operational processes. Organizations should be led and managed so that innovation becomes part of the learning culture. Innovation should be integrated into daily work and should be supported by your performance improvement system.

Innovation builds on the accumulated knowledge of your organization and its faculty and staff. Therefore, the ability to rapidly disseminate and capitalize on this knowledge is critical to driving organizational innovation.

Management by Fact

Organizations depend on the measurement and analysis of performance. Such measurements should derive from the organization's needs and strategy, and they should provide critical data and information about key processes and results. Many types of data and information are needed for performance management. Performance measurement should focus on student learning, which requires a comprehensive and integrated fact-based system—one that includes input data, environmental data, performance data, comparative/competitive data, data on faculty and staff, cost data, and operational performance measurement. Measurement areas might include students' backgrounds, learning styles, aspirations, academic strengths and weaknesses, educational progress, classroom and program learning, satisfaction with instruction and services, extracurricular activities, dropout/matriculation rates, and postgraduation success. Examples of appropriate data segmentation include segmentation by student learning results, student demographics, and faculty and staff groups.

Analysis refers to extracting larger meaning from data and information to support evaluation, decision making, and improvement. Analysis entails using data to determine trends, projections, and cause and effect that might not otherwise be evident. Analysis supports a variety of purposes, such as planning, reviewing your overall performance, improving operations, accomplishing change management, and comparing your performance with organizations providing similar programs and services or with "best practices" benchmarks.

A major consideration in performance improvement and change management involves the selection and use of performance measures or indicators. *The measures or indicators you select should best represent the factors that lead to improved student, operational, financial, and ethical performance. A comprehensive set of measures or indicators tied to student, stakeholder, and organizational performance requirements represents a clear basis for aligning all processes with your organization's goals.* Through the analysis of data from your tracking processes, your measures or indicators themselves may be evaluated and changed to better support your goals.

Social Responsibility

An organization's leaders should stress responsibilities to the public, ethical behavior, and the need to practice good citizenship. Leaders should be role models for your organization in focusing on ethics and protection of public health, safety, and the environment. Protection of health, safety, and the environment includes your organization's operations. Planning should anticipate adverse impacts that might arise in facilities management, laboratory operations, and transportation. Effective planning should prevent problems, provide for a forthright response if problems occur, and make available information and support needed to maintain public awareness, safety, and confidence.

Organizations should not only meet all local, state, and federal laws and regulatory requirements, but they should treat these and related requirements as opportunities for improvement "beyond mere compliance." Organizations should stress ethical behavior in all stakeholder transactions and interactions. Highly ethical conduct should be a requirement of and should be monitored by the organization's governance body.

Practicing good citizenship refers to leadership and support—within the limits of an organization's resources—of publicly important purposes. Such purposes might include improving education in your community, pursuing environmental excellence, practicing resource conservation, performing community service, and sharing quality-related information. Leadership also entails influencing other organizations, private and public, to partner for these purposes.

Managing social responsibility requires the use of appropriate measures and leadership responsibility for those measures.

Focus on Results and Creating Value

An organization's performance measurements need to focus on key results. Results should be used to create and balance value for your students and for your key stakeholders—the community, parents, employers, faculty and staff, suppliers, partners, and the public. By creating value for students and stakeholders, your organization contributes to society and to improving overall education performance, and it builds loyalty. To meet the sometimes conflicting and changing aims that balancing value implies, organizational strategy explicitly should include key stakeholder requirements. This will help ensure that plans and actions meet differing stakeholder needs and avoid adverse impacts on any stakeholders. The use of a balanced composite of leading and lagging performance measures offers an effective means to communicate short- and longer-term priorities, monitor actual performance, and provide a clear basis for improving results.

Systems Perspective

The Baldrige Criteria provide a systems perspective for managing your organization and its key processes to achieve results—performance excellence. The seven Baldrige Categories and the Core Values form the building blocks and the integrating mechanism for the system. However, successful management of overall performance requires organization-specific synthesis, alignment, and integration. Synthesis means looking at your organization as a whole and builds on key educational requirements, including your strategic objectives and action plans. Alignment means using the key linkages among requirements given in the Baldrige Categories to ensure consistency of plans, processes, measures, and actions. Integration builds on alignment so that the individual components of your performance management system operate in a fully interconnected manner.

These concepts are depicted in the Baldrige framework (see Figure 29). A systems perspective includes your senior leaders' focus on strategic direc-

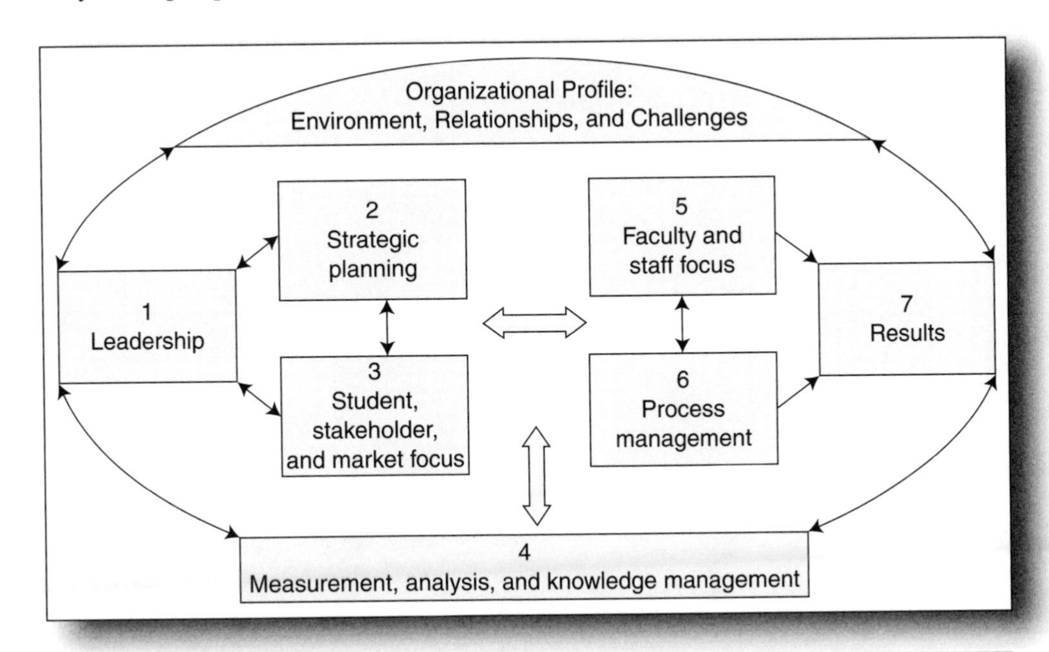

Figure 29 Baldrige framework.

tions and on your students and stakeholders. It means that your senior leaders monitor, respond to, and manage performance based on your results. A systems perspective also includes using your measures, indicators, and organizational knowledge to build your key strategies. It means linking these strategies with your key processes and aligning your resources to improve overall performance and satisfy students and stakeholders.

Thus, a systems perspective means managing your whole organization, as well as its components, to achieve success.

Helpful Resources

BOOKS

ABS Consulting. 2005. *Root Cause Analysis Handbook: A Guide to Effective Incident Investigation.* Brookfield, CT: Rothstein Associates.

Alexander, William F., and Richard W. Serfas. 1999. *Futuring Tools for Strategic Quality Planning in Education.* Milwaukee, WI: ASQ Quality Press.

Alstete, Jeffrey W. 1996. *Benchmarking in Higher Education: Adapting Best Practices to Improve Quality.* Washington, DC: NACUBO.

Andersen, Bjørn, and Tom Fagerhaug. 2006. *Root Cause Analysis: Simplified Tools and Techniques.* 2nd ed. Milwaukee, WI: ASQ Quality Press.

APQC. 2003. *A Guide to Reinventing Schools* [the Chugach, Alaska Model]. Houston, TX: American Productivity and Quality Center.

———. 2004. *Educators in Action: Examining Strategic Improvement Efforts.* Houston, TX: American Productivity and Quality Center.

APQC Passport to [Education] Success Series. 2000. *Benchmarking Best Practices in Accountability Systems.* Houston, TX: American Productivity and Quality Center.

———. 2002. *Benchmarking: A Guide for Your Journey to Best-Practice Processes.* Houston, TX: American Productivity and Quality Center.

ASQ Koalaty Kid. 2003. *School Self-Assessment Guide for Performance Excellence.* Milwaukee, WI: ASQ Quality Press.

ASQ Quality Education Division. 2003. *Successful Applications of Quality Systems in K–12 Schools.* Milwaukee, WI: ASQ Quality Press.

ASQ Quality Management Division, John E. Bauer, Grace L. Duffy, and Russell T. Westcott, eds. 2006. *The Quality Improvement Handbook.* 2nd ed. Milwaukee, WI: ASQ Quality Press.

Bernhardt, Victoria L. 2004. *Data Analysis for Continuous School Improvement.* Larchmont, NY: Eye on Education.

Blazey, Mark, et al. 2006. *Insights to Performance Excellence in Education 2006: An Inside Look at the 2006 Baldrige Award Criteria for Education.* Milwaukee, WI: ASQ Quality Press.

Brown, Mark Graham. 2006. *The Pocket Guide to the Baldrige Award Criteria.* 12th ed. Milwaukee, WI: ASQ Quality Press.

Byrnes, Margaret A., with Jeanne C. Baxter. 2005. *There Is Another Way!: Launch a Baldrige-Based Quality Classroom.* Milwaukee, WI: ASQ Quality Press.

———. 2006. *The Principal's Leadership Counts! Launch a Baldrige-Based Quality School.* Milwaukee, WI: ASQ Quality Press.

Collins, Jim. 2001. *Good to Great.* New York: Harper Collins.

Conyers, John G., and Robert Ewy. 2004. *Charting Your Course: Lessons Learned during the Journey toward Performance Excellence.* Milwaukee, WI: ASQ Quality Press.

Conzemius, Anne, and Jan O'Neill. 2005. *The Power of SMART Goals: Using Goals to Improve Student Learning.* Milwaukee, WI: ASQ Quality Press.

Davenport, Patricia, and Gerald Anderson. 2002. *Closing the Achievement Gap: No Excuses.* Houston, TX: American Productivity and Quality Center.

Deming, W. Edwards. 1994. *The New Economics: For Industry, Government, Education.* 2nd ed. Cambridge, MA: Massachusetts Institute of Technology, Center for Advanced Engineering Study.

Harry, Mikel, and Richard Schroeder. 2006. *Six Sigma: The Breakthrough Management Strategy Revolutionizing the World's Top Corporations.* New York: Random House.

Jenkins, Lee. 2003. *Improving Student Learning: Applying Deming's Quality Principles in the Classroom.* 2nd ed. Milwaukee, WI: ASQ Quality Press.

———. 2004. *Permission to Forget: And Nine Other Root Causes of America's Frustration with Education.* Milwaukee, WI: ASQ Quality Press.

Leavitt, Paige, Randy McDaniel, and Emma Skogstad. 2004. *Disaggregating Data in Schools.* Houston, TX: American Productivity and Quality Center.

Marzano, Robert J. 2003. *What Works in Schools: Translating Research into Action.* Alexandria, VA: Association for Supervision and Curriculum Development (ASCD).

Massy, William F. 2003. *Honoring the Trust: Quality and Cost Containment in Higher Education.* Boston: Anker Publishing Company.

Maurer, Richard, and Sandra Cokeley-Pedersen. 2004. *Malcolm and Me.* Lanham, MD: Scarecrow Press.

Ott, Ellis R., Edward G. Schilling, and Dean V. Neubauer. 2005. *Process Quality Control: Troubleshooting and Interpretation of Data.* 4th ed. Milwaukee, WI: ASQ Quality Press.

Palmer, Brian. 2004. *Making Change Work: Practical Tools for Overcoming Human Resistance to Change.* Milwaukee, WI: ASQ Quality Press.

Peterson, R. A. 2000. *Constructing Effective Questionnaires.* Thousand Oaks, CA: SAGE Publications.

Preuss, P. G. 2003. *School Leader's Guide to Root Cause Analysis: Using Data to Dissolve Problems.* Larchmont, NY: Eye on Education.

ReVelle, Jack B. 2004. *Quality Essentials: A Reference Guide from A to Z.* Milwaukee, WI: ASQ Quality Press.

Ruben, Brent D. 2003. *Pursuing Excellence in Higher Education: Eight Fundamental Challenges.* Washington, DC: NACUBO.

———. 2005. *Excellence in Higher Education: An Integrated Approach to Assessment, Planning, and Improvement in Colleges and Universities.* Washington, DC: NACUBO.

———. 2005. *Excellence in Higher Education: An Integrated Approach to Assessment, Planning, and Improvement Workbook and Scoring Guide.* Washington, DC: NACUBO.

Simon, A. R. 1998. *Data Warehousing for Dummies.* Foster City, CA: IDG Books Worldwide.

Sorensen, Charles W., Julie A. Furst-Bowe, and Diane M. Moen, eds. 2005. *Quality and Performance Excellence in Higher Education: Baldrige on Campus.* Boston: Anker Publishing Company.

Tromp, Sherrie A., and Brent D. Ruben. 2004. *Strategic Planning in Higher Education: A Guide for Leaders.* Washington, DC: NACUBO.

Wheeler, Donald. 2003. *Making Sense of Data.* Knoxville, TN: SPC Press.

Zemsky, Robert, Gregory R. Wegner, and William F. Massy. 2005. *Remaking the American University: Market-Smart and Mission-Centered.* Piscataway, NJ: Rutgers University Press.

Quality Tools Books

Arthur, Jay. 2000. *Six Sigma Simplified: Quantum Improvement Made Easy.* Denver, CO: LifeStar.

GOAL/QPC and Joiner Associates. 1995. *The Team Memory Jogger: A Pocket Guide for Team Members.* Salem, NH: GOAL/QPC.

Kingery, Cathy, ed. 2002. *The Six Sigma Memory Jogger II.* Salem, NH: GOAL/QPC.

McManus, Ann (adapted by). 1992. *The Memory Jogger for Education: A Pocket Guide of Tools for Continuous Improvement in Schools.* Salem, NH: GOAL/QPC.

Oddo, Francine, ed. 1994. *The Memory Jogger II.* Salem, NH: GOAL/QPC.

Ritter, Diane, and Michael Brassard. 1998. *The Creativity Tools Memory Jogger.* Salem, NH: GOAL/QPC.

Tague, Nancy R. 2004. *The Quality Toolbox.* 2nd ed. Milwaukee, WI: ASQ Quality Press.

WEB SITES

Baldrige Materials

American Society for Quality
http://www.asq.org
Obtain multiple copies of the Criteria

Baldrige National Quality Program
http://www.baldrige.gov
Obtain a free copy of the following:

- *Are We Making Progress? (Employees)*
- *Are We Making Progress? (Leaders)*
- *Education Criteria Booklet*
- *E-Baldrige Self-Assessment and Action Planning Profile for Education*
- *Getting Started with the Baldrige Criteria for Performance Excellence*

http://www.baldrige.gov/Award_Recipients.htm
Download previous winners' applications and profiles

Baldrige Education Award Recipients

Chugach Schools, Anchorage, AK
http://www.chugachschools.com

Community Consolidated School District 15, Palatine, IL
http://www.ccsd15.k12.il.us

Jenks Public Schools, Jenks, OK
http://www.jenksps.org

Kenneth W. Monfort College of Business at UNC, Greeley, CO
http://www.mcb.unco.edu/

Pearl River School District, Pearl River, NY
http://www.pearlriver.k12.ny.us

Richland College, Dallas, TX
http://www.richlandcollege.edu

University of Wisconsin-Stout, Menomonie, WI
http://www.uwstout.edu

Benchmarking

Aldine ISD
http://www.aldine.k12.tx.us
Benchmark its support services in a district of more than 54,000 students—55 percent Latino, 34 percent Black, and 9 percent Anglo.

APPA—Association of Higher Education Facilities Officers
http://www.appa.org
Dedicated to the maintenance, protection, and promotion of quality education facilities.

APQC—Process Improvement & Implementation in Education (PIIE) Benchmarking Program
http://www.apqc.org/site/educ/sitemap.html

Benchmarking Network
http://www.benchmarkingnetwork.com
Sign up for a free newsletter.

EnergyStar
http://www.energystar.gov/index.cfm?c=assess_performance.benchmark
Allows you to benchmark use of energy for facilities with like institutions around the country.

State Education Initiatives

California—CA Center for Baldrige in Education
http://www.qualityineducation.org

Illinois—Business Roundtable
http://www.baldrigeineducation.org

New Mexico—Strengthening Quality in Schools
http://www.sandia.gov/sqs

North Carolina—NC Business Committee for Education
http://www.ncbce.org

Assessments and Surveys

Brainchild OLA
http://www.brainchild.com
Online assessments aligned with state standards in math and reading.

CSMPact School Satisfaction Survey
mgosney@harrisinteractive.com
Contact: Michelle Gosney

Futuristics Research
http://www.futuristicsresearch.com
Alumni and other satisfaction survey services. Contact: Tucker Pierce.

National Association of College and University Business Officers
http://www.nacubo.org/documents/business_topics/organizational_checklist.pdf

Southwest Educational Development Laboratory
http://www.sedl.org/pitl/rci/rad/
Information and reading assessments for pre-K through third grade in multiple languages.

SPSS
http://www.spss.com/index.htm
A leading worldwide provider of predictive analytics software and solutions.

SurveyShare.com
http://www.surveyshare.com/resources/
Information on how to write surveys, along with survey templates that can be adapted for your use. Free membership.

Techniques for Writing Surveys
http://www.lhs.logan.k12.ut.us/~jsmart/survey/page3.html

Data Collection, Measurement, and Analysis

Business Process Improvement
http://www.spcforexcel.com

QI Macros
http://www.qimacros.com

Six Sigma
http://www.isixsigma.com

Baldrige-Related Topics

American Society for Quality
http://www.asq.org/communities/baldrige-education
Baldrige in Education networking.

International Center for Leadership in Education
http://www.daggett.com/about_matrix.html
Learn about the Curriculum Matrix developed by Dr. Willard Daggett and his associates and alignment to your state standards.

National Consortium for Continuous Improvement in Higher Education
http://www.ncci-cu.org

National School Boards Association: The Keywork of School Boards Guidebook
http://www.nsba.org/site/page.asp?TRACKID=&CID=121&DID=8799

Strategic Planning

Charity Village
http://www.charityvillage.com/cv/research/rstrat17.html

TEC
http://www.teconline.com/www/bestpratices/strategic_planning.asp

Succession Planning—Career Path Definition

Best Practices
http://www3.best-in-class.com

Potential Sources for Funding Baldrige Training

Federal Funds Express
http://www.house.gov/ffr/resources_all.shtml

Internet Prospector
http://www.internet-prospector.org/found.html

State Quality Award Web Sites

Alabama Quality Award
http://www.alabamaproductivitycenter.com

Arizona State Quality Award Program
http://www.arizona-excellence.com

Arkansas Performance Excellence Awards
http://www.arkansasexcellence.org

California Awards for Performance Excellence
http://www.calexcellence.org

Colorado—Excellence in Customer Service Award
http://www.bbbsc.org

Connecticut Breakthrough Quality Award
http://www.ctqualityaward.org

Florida—Governor's Sterling Award
http://www.floridasterling.com

Georgia Focus Recognition
http://www.georgiaoglethorpe.org

Hawaii State Award of Excellence
http://www.cochawaii.org

Idaho Quality Award
http://www.idahoworks.com

Illinois—The Lincoln Foundation for Achievement of Excellence
http://www.lincolnaward.org

Iowa Recognition for Performance Excellence
http://www.iowaqc.org

Kansas Award for Excellence Program
http://kae.bluestep.net

Commonwealth of Kentucky Quality Award
http://www.kqc.org

Massachusetts Performance Excellence Award
http://www.massexcellence.com

Michigan Quality Leadership Award
http://www.michiganquality.org

Minnesota Quality Award
http://www.councilforquality.org

Mississippi Quality Awards Program
http://www.sbcjc.cc.ms.us

Missouri Quality Award
http://www.mqa.org

Nebraska—Edgerton Quality Awards
http://assist.neded.org/edgerton

Nevada—APEX Nevada State Quality Award
http://www.nvqa.org

New Hampshire—Granite State Quality Award
http://www.gsqc.com

New Jersey—Governor's Award for Performance Excellence
http://www.gnj.org

The New Mexico Quality Awards
http://www.qualitynewmexico.org

New York—The Governor's Award for Excellence
http://www.empirestateadvantage.org

North Carolina Awards for Excellence
http://www.ies.ncsu.edu/qualityaward

The Ohio Award for Excellence
http://www.partnershipohio.org

Oklahoma Quality Award
http://www.oklahomaquality.com

Pennsylvania—The Lancaster Chamber Excellence Award
http://www.lancasterchamber.com/excellence

Rhode Island Award for Competence and Performance Excellence
http://www.ricpe.org

South Carolina Governor's Quality Award
http://www.scquality.com

Tennessee Excellence Award
http://www.tncpe.org

Texas Award for Performance Excellence
http://www.texas-quality.org

Vermont Program for Performance Excellence
http://www.vermontquality.org

Virginia—U.S. Senate Productivity and Quality Award
http://www.spqa-va.org/quality

Washington State Quality Award
http://www.wsqa.net

Wisconsin Forward Award
http://www.forwardaward.org

Other Resources

Baldrige in Education Collaboration Project
http://www.baldrigeineducation.org
Sponsored by the Illinois Business Roundtable and NCREL

RISC ReInventing Schools Coalition
http://www.reinventingschools.org

Index

D

E

F

G

I

J

K

L

M

N

O

P

R

S

T

U

V